Story, Text, and Scripture
Literary Interests in Biblical Narrative

Also by Wesley A. Kort

Shriven Selves: Religious Problems in Recent American Fiction (1972)
Narrative Elements and Religious Meaning (1975)
Moral Fiber: Character and Belief in Recent American Fiction (1982)
Modern Fiction and Human Time: A Study in Narrative and Belief (1985)

STORY, TEXT, and SCRIPTURE

Literary Interests in Biblical Narrative

WESLEY A. KORT

THE PENNSYLVANIA STATE UNIVERSITY PRESS
University Park and London

Library of Congress Cataloging-in-Publication Data
Kort, Wesley A.
Story, text, and scripture.

Bibliography: p.
Includes index.
1. Narration in the Bible. 2. Bible—Criticism
interpretation, etc.—History—20th century.
3. Bible as literature. I. Title.
BS537.K67   1987   220.6'6   87-42549
ISBN 0-271-00610-2

For
Cal, Hank, and Jo

Contents

Preface

This book arose from two sources. The first was a request from a group of graduate students in biblical studies several years ago asking me to offer a seminar that would treat some of the recent literary interests in biblical narratives. This request constituted a challenge because these students, well trained in linguistic, textual, and historical methods, were conditioned to greet these newer efforts with mild impatience or outright disdain. I accepted their invitation knowing that, if literary interests would impress them as worth taking seriously, I could not disregard or denigrate the genuine insights into the material that their own training provided them. The challenge and excitement of the seminar encouraged me to continue with the project, and this book would not exist had it not been for those students.

The other source was my own scholarly interests. As may be clear from my earlier work, I take the relation of religion to literature to rest on the interdependence between religious meaning and literary form. This addresses two questions: Why do traditional societies commonly pass down and receive their sacred traditions in narrative form? And do narratives today continue to be bearers of religious meaning? Although I have spent most of my time working on the second of these questions, the relation of narrative to belief as that is recognizable in recent literature, the other is always in my mind. And I welcomed the chance to pursue it.

The first matter to settle, in preparing for the seminar, was orga-
nization, since I agree with Northrop Frye that it is not literature
that is taught so much as a framework for understanding it. This
meant that I could not present a syllabus that merely listed a number of recent literary studies of biblical texts without accounting for
their differences. Some reason had to be given for difference itself.
To study recent literary interests in biblical narrative is to encounter a range of methods and approaches, and accounting for that
variety is a fundamental theoretical task. This task led to my proposal that narrative itself, because of its complex form, attracts
interpretations and theoretical reflection that primarily address
one or another of its various aspects. Consequently, narrative theories or literary interests provide a way of talking about narrative's
complexity. The narrative form itself, therefore, provides unity
amidst the plurality of critical voices. This proposal organized the
seminar, and the eventual result constitutes the central chapter of
this book.

But two matters, more fundamental and more controversial, had
to be undertaken as well, and at those points the going was more
difficult, since I could not count on the help of literary critics and
theorists. At issue, first of all, is the status or role of narrative in
human life and experience. For reasons I shall suggest later, people
tend to think of narrative as derivative and optional. Both biblical
scholars and literary critics appear to take narrative as dependent
upon more basic matters, such as facts and beliefs, or events and
ideas. They understand narrative to be an unsteady compound that
asks to be broken down into its original components. A minority
voice is beginning to speak against that notion and the prevailing
epistemologies that support it, and in this book I add my voice to
this countertone.

The second issue concerns textuality. We also tend, for reasons
equally attributable to prevailing epistemologies, to denigrate the
importance of texts. Consequently, the nature of biblical narratives
as texts must also be taken up. With help from Jacques Derrida (but
also in opposition to him), our position in the world as a textual one
is described, and the question of scripture is placed in this textual
situation.

I was willing to press the need to take narrative textuality as
fundamental to human life, even though the students requesting
the seminar did not have this issue in mind. Frankly, it struck me as
the most urgent matter of all. Custodians of narrative texts should

not compromise the fundamental characteristics of the material. Required is the recognition that the religious meaning of the material is generated first of all because of features constitutive to its fundamental nature as narrative and text. The religious meaning and significance of biblical material and its literary and textual form are inseparable.

Lurking in the background, I finally realized, was an old issue, one I thought I had left behind for other people to worry about, namely, a doctrine of scripture. In a word, it is not surprising that this religious datum, sacred writ, should have such an awkward position in our time, given the low view we tend to have both of narrative and of textuality. The last pages of this book, then, present a propaedeutic to a religious understanding of narrative texts as scripture.

The second of the two questions concerning literature and religion—do literary texts written in our own day carry religious meaning?—although subordinate in this study, cannot, in the concluding comments, be fully suppressed. For if it is true that the religious meaning of "sacred" texts is inseparable from literary and textual characteristics, it is also true that literary texts, which we assume to be "secular," inevitably bear or generate meanings of religious significance. Consequently, it is possible to develop, in relation to them, a doctrine of scripture as well. I shall conclude, therefore, with the comment that the "sacred" and "secular" scriptures are not so different as we may think them to be; the distinction is based less on the nature of the texts than on the interests of the differing communities charged with their keep.

Parts of this book, especially the first two chapters, were presented in differing forms elsewhere. "Literatur und Theologie," a lecture I gave at the University of Bonn, draws from these chapters, and it appeared later as an essay in *Stimmen der Zeit.* I am grateful to Professor Gerhard Sauter, my host at Bonn, to Professor Johannes Brosseder, who helped me with the translation of the lecture into German, and to Fr. Wolfgang Seibel, editor of *Stimmen der Zeit,* for their interest in my work. My essay "Narrative and Theology," also based on the opening chapters of this book, appeared in the first number of *Literature and Theology,* a journal published by Oxford University Press and edited by Dr. David Jasper, director of the new Center for the Study of Literature and Theology at the University of Durham, England. I am deeply grateful to him for the friendship our mutual interests have helped create. Finally, I gave a paper at a conference of the International Religious Foundation, and that paper resembles the present second chapter. I am grateful to all of these organizations and persons for permission to reuse this material.

I want, in conclusion, to thank a number of friends and colleagues who have read all or parts of the manuscript and who have encouraged me, by their interest in my work, far more than they may realize and far more than I can adequately acknowledge: Kalman Bland, my colleague in Religion here at Duke; David Rhoads, of Carthage College; Mary Fulkerson and Tom Langford, both of Duke's Divinity faculty; Fred Horton, of Wake Forest University; and Conrad Ostwalt, my graduate assistant.

Wesley A. Kort
Duke University
Spring 1987

Introduction

Literary interests will change, perhaps already have changed, our understanding of biblical texts in general and of biblical narratives in particular. Rather than simply adding something to other interests or standing as an alternative to them, literary interests actually or potentially alter the status of biblical material and, consequently, our relation to and understanding of it. To put the matter as boldly as possible: Literary interests in biblical narratives require or imply a new concept of scripture.

This new concept will have the advantage of being based on considerations arising from qualities inherent to the material rather than from interests brought to it from some other source. These basic qualities are narrativity and textuality. The principal assumption directing the argument of this book, then, is that the texts of biblical narratives themselves reveal properties that both require a new concept of scripture and adumbrate what kind of concept that should be.

The choice of narrativity as one of the two defining characteristics of biblical material requires defense, since many literary forms are present in the collections of texts that constitute Hebrew and Christian Scriptures: lyrical, legal, proverbial, epistolary, and many more. Indeed, these forms, rather than in isolation from one another, should be taken together as mutually clarifying and complicating. But narrative has a certain primacy because it provides biblical material with its particular coherence. Within this narrative coherence the other forms take their places or produce their particular kinds of tensions. However, while narrative is given a place of privilege here, the possibility of a lyrical or dramatic coherence for biblical material should be recognized. Since the narratives are so heavy with evaluation—with feeling, let us say—they have a certain lyrical or confessional quality, and this quality could be taken, along with the more noticeably lyrical books or passages, as providing coherence. The line between prose and poetry, between the narrative and the lyrical, in biblical texts is not always easy to draw or maintain. Nor should it be thought of as totally out of the question to treat biblical material as having a certain dramatic or liturgical coherence. Not only is this possibility indicated by the kinds of settings that form criticism reveals texts originally to have had in the liturgical life of people; it is also indicated by the continuing liturgical use of the texts in the worship of Jews and Christians throughout their histories and into the present day. One has no basis for arguing that a dramatic or liturgical coherence is an imposition on the material. Indeed, the material seems itself often to call for a liturgical context and to be inherently dramatic.

Despite the legitimate claims of a lyrical and a dramatic coherence, narrative nudges out the other two major forms for two reasons. One is that, despite lacunae and reversals, the narratives provide a whole that can easily be apprehended together in its temporal arrangement. (For the Christian Bible this temporal arrangement is, as Northrop Frye stresses, quite complete, from Creation to Apocalypse.) Perhaps more important, in our time the Bible, whatever one might include or not include in that collection, is something to be read more than something to be sung or staged, and reading means, at a minimal level, starting at a beginning and moving on to an ending, with everything in between finding some place or other in that temporal coherence.

The choice of textuality as a basic characteristic of the material may not need to be defended. Again taking a minimal position, we can say that in dealing with biblical material we confront writing, script. Of course, one could press the issue that the print is an occasion for voice or performance, and a lyrical or dramatic coherence would not so quickly posit textuality as a basic characteristic of biblical material. But the same pressures that push biblical narrativity to the fore as a basic characteristic do the same for textuality. A concept of scripture in our time, then, should work with two determining characteristics of biblical material, its narrativity and its textuality. Whatever else the material may be or become, it is first of all narrative text. These two qualities form the foundation for the altered concept of scripture that literary interests provide.

Literary interests, therefore, do not impose themselves on the religious meaning or theological standing of biblical material. Rather, if there are religious and theological meanings and force in biblical narratives, they derive from and can be traced to the characteristics of narrativity and textuality. It is not as though narrative and text are neutral containers or occasions for a religious or theological content and agenda. Religious meaning does not antedate and cannot be divorced from narrativity and textuality. The literary and religious are fundamentally joined. To put it another way, if the Bible reveals something about religion and about God, it does so in and through narrativity and textuality. A concept of scripture such as here proposed, therefore, has a literary base before it has a theological consequence.

A corollary of this study is that a literary doctrine of scripture also implies a more scriptural doctrine of literature. That is, if it is true that the religious force and meaning of biblical narratives are fundamentally to be related to formal and textual properties, then it follows that so-called secular literature has a moral and spiritual, let us say religious, standing that actually or potentially is more important than now generally recognized. To put it another way, if literary studies can help us to understand how religious meaning and power are generated in and by a biblical text, a study of biblical narratives will help us to recognize that the literary venture is never dissociated from value and belief and is never, consequently, far from religion.

Readers with religious and theological interests likely will demur when told that a concept of scripture can and should be built upon the literary characteristics of narrativity and textuality. They have behind them what appears to be the unanimous support of theologians that "scripture" is a theological and not a literary concept. But this position, I shall argue, stands on an underestimation or miscalculation of the nature, function, and status both of narrative as a form of discourse and of textuality. It is only after a reassessment of narrative and of text that the propositions fundamental to this study can begin to carry weight.

Readers with literary interests may demur when I advance the corollary that the religious and theological meaning and standing of biblical narratives reveal something about narrativity and textuality more generally. Literary theory and criticism counter this proposal because the consequence, if not the intention, of literary studies has been to demystify and secularize literary texts. Despite pauses and detours in that process, we are poised today before a literary situation in which the spirits, not only divine but human as well, will be fully routed from the literary temple, its walls leveled, and its stones offered as toys for purposeless play.

The doctrine of scripture that I am proposing, then, is an alternative to religious interests that inadequately appreciate narrativity and textuality and to literary interests that fail to acknowledge the religious implications of narrativity and textuality. The appearance of God in narrative, textual form, I shall argue, challenges attempts to talk about religion without also addressing narrativity and textuality. Conversely, I shall argue that the appearance of God in narrative form does not establish such texts as discontinuous with other narratives, as, for example, Northrop Frye, Mikhail Bakhtin, and Frank Kermode, in their varying ways, would say, but rather that it reveals the nature, function, and status of all narratives. The appearance of God in narrative form reveals something about narrative as well as about God. My goal is to move literary matters to the center of religious studies, and, at the same time, to allow the religious significance of literary studies to appear. For just as a religious doctrine of scripture has a literary base, literary studies have a scriptural consequence, a consequence, that is, not only for an understanding of biblical narratives but also for an understanding of the scriptural role of "secular" texts, narratives whose unavoidable engagement with the spiritual may be concealed or repressed either by them or by their interpreters.

Although both narrativity and textuality are central to the study, I must begin with one and defer the other to the end. The order I have chosen could—perhaps should—be reversed. In any event, no priority is intended by this arrangement. The reasons for it are prudential. While there is no consensus concerning the nature, function, and status of narrative—indeed, I take exception to almost all that is currently being said about these matters—the topic itself is less controversial. Textuality and the attendant topics of "writing" and "canon" are provocative, if not volatile, topics. In addition, including with them, as I do, the term "scripture" intensifies an already charged atmosphere. Caution dictates, therefore, that I begin with narrativity and defer textuality to the end.

Even less should the placement of narrativity at the outset and textuality at the end be interpreted as exposing a gap or lag between them. Indeed, the two cannot be discussed apart. However, the issues appropriate to each are separable. As there is no priority implied by first and last, there is no implicit separation between the two. Narrativity always implies textuality, and textuality always implies narrativity.

Placed between these two theoretical chapters are three with a more practical emphasis. The first of these, Chapter 2, offers an analysis and interpretation of four biblical narratives: Exodus, Judges, Jonah, and the Gospel According to Mark. The purpose of this chapter is to provide illustrations or experimental samples for the more theoretical issues here addressed. Consequently, I do not attempt to address all the scholarly problems these narratives present or to survey the voluminous scholarship concerning them. This use of them is not abuse, however, because the issues central to this study are also integral to the examples, to their narrative and textual characteristics.

The third chapter is a study of prominent literary methods now in use for the analysis and interpretation of biblical narrative. My purpose is not only to describe each of these methods and to extend them to the four examples but also to display the limitations of these methods, the nature of those limitations, and the cause of them. That is, I shall point out that the strengths of these methods rest on their limitations, that the strengthening of the method is done at the expense of the narrative form. Each method, I shall argue, consequently serves itself as much as narrative. The nature of narrative, which the four biblical examples reveal, indicates the limitations of the critical methods.

The last of the middle chapters, 4, moves the methods and the narrative examples to questions of textuality. The methods, we shall see, rest as much on textuality as on narrativity, and they reveal the characteristics of textuality.

The final chapter deals with textuality, the second of the central issues in this study. The first objective is to clarify the distinction, even the Scylla-and-Charybdis-like gap, between "writing" and "canon." I shall propose between them a concept of "scripture." The central question here concerns centrality or orientation in the textual field. I shall then go on to say why biblical texts grant us a model of what a scripture ought to be like, primarily in its ability to decenter as well as center. In the Conclusion I shall recommend a literary concept of scripture to religious interests in the Bible, and I shall suggest that "secular" literature also plays a scriptural role and should be accordingly interpreted and evaluated.

1

Narrative:
A Reassessment

Before narrativity can be taken into account as a characteristic of biblical discourse fundamental to its scriptural possibilities, prevalent assumptions concerning narrative must be challenged. These assumptions concern not only the nature of narrative but also its function and status. The separation of religious from literary and literary from religious interests arises not so much from a separation between religious narratives and secular ones or between the narratives of religiously defined cultures and the narratives of our own as from assumptions we have concerning narrative, assumptions closely tied to our self-understandings, to our attitudes as denizens of the modern West. By means of these assumptions we tend to denigrate narrative as a form of discourse, and this denigration sets us not only apart but also, it seems, above other peoples and periods. To challenge such assumptions, therefore, is not only to go against the stream but also to engage in a kind of self-subversion that will always be incomplete. But our assumptions, even if they cannot be altered completely and finally, may, at least for a moment, be checked. And when they are we will share a glimpse of what it would mean to have a literary doctrine of scripture, a doctrine, that is, neither based on an abstraction of the religious from the literary nor eschewed by literary interests and endeavors.

Whether by neglect or malice, our understanding of and appreciation for narrative have seriously eroded. This may appear to be an inaccurate diagnosis of the state of narrative in current scholarship. Indeed, we seem to stand amidst an outpouring of studies that have the nature, status, or function of narrative either as their central foci or as important ancillary concerns. However, this scholarship largely tends to reinforce rather than to challenge habits of thought, with damaging consequences for our assessments of and attitudes toward narrative. Nor can it be said that the current interests among biblical scholars in literary criticism and theory amend the situation, for such interests are dependent upon the orientations of the literary field. In order to address the impact of narrativity as a characteristic of biblical texts, we must begin with a reassessment of narrative itself.

The reassessment can be undertaken by addressing three questions. The first concerns the status of narrative. Is narrative a derivative and secondary form of discourse, or is it primary and originating? Of course, no final answer can be given to such a question, but it is important to understand that we tend to assume that narrative is derivative and secondary. There are compelling epistemological reasons for this assumption. We should recognize them in order to entertain the notion that narrative may be a primary and originating form of discourse. The second question concerns the nature of narrative. Is it a steady, centered or centering form of discourse, or is it varying and decentering? This question addresses the tendency in narrative theory and criticism to simplify the form and to assume that it is always the same. We should recognize that narrative is complex rather than simple and varying rather than steady. The third question concerns the function of narrative. While many functions have been and can be cited for narrative discourse, the one crucial to this study— narrative as a bearer of belief—is, for reasons to be discussed, neglected, and the consequence of the neglect is an unfortunate and untenable separation between the literary and the religious. I will propose that narrative discourse stands between ordinary discourse and questions concerning human life that cannot be answered apart from beliefs. To put it more sharply, narrative stands between discourse and mystery. "Religious" narratives are those that either draw attention to "mystery" or have traditionally been read in ways that suppress the literary for the sake of the mystery. "Secular" narratives are those that either draw attention to literary properties or have traditionally been read in ways that suppress their engagement with mystery for the sake of those properties.

The Status of Narrative

When we assume that narrative is occasional, optional, and derivative, we jeopardize an appreciation and understanding of biblical narrative and make impossible a concept of scripture based in part on narrativity. A reassessment of narrative's status is needed. This can be accomplished by entertaining the contrary possibility, namely, that narrative, instead, is ubiquitous, necessary, and primary.

Narratives are always and everywhere to be found. This ubiquity of narrative is no small or simply curious matter. As the American philosopher of history Hayden White suggests, the study of a culture's narratives is an inquiry that quickly becomes a study of culture, even of humanity, itself.[1] That is, students of narrative, when they encounter cultural historians or other social scientists, may find that the object of their study is taken more seriously by others than they themselves are prepared to take it. Deferring other implications of such testimony, let us consider only the implications of ubiquity.

For one thing, it means that ancient people, such as those from among whom biblical texts originated, are like us and are available to us not only because of the textuality that allows the gap between our culture and theirs to be bridged but also because of the narrative form. That is, narrative undercuts the distances and differences, however great they may be, between cultures, so that the culture of ancient Israel, different and distant from our own in so many respects, is also joined to our own in this way. It is important to recognize that, in addition to sharing an orientation to texts, we share a single base: the narrative form. This says something far more complex and more precise than to say we share with people different and distant from us the common need for culture and a common humanity. With all the necessary stress on cultural differences and all of the distancing that historicism produces between our own time and that of people of the past, it is a matter of no small importance to recognize this shared base, to emphasize the ubiquity of narrative.

Narrative's ubiquity also calls for a reassessment of the relation of the narrative form to language, one I shall clarify more fully later on. We tend to think that narrative arises from language. Since language differences present barriers between peoples and limits to the extent of their ability to understand one another, the narratives of a people, when viewed as products of language, are placed at a second stage of removal and become strange lands to us. But the ubiquity of narrative may allow a reversal of this assumption. It becomes possible to say that, rather than arising from language, narrative is either coexistent with the origination of language or, in some way or other, even itself the originator of language. In any event, along with the obvious distances created between us and peoples with differing languages, narrative as a shared form of discourse grants a potential access to them. While we do not have the same language as other peoples and differ from them in customs, mores, and values, we need not treat others as an array of relatively autonomous isles, with passage to them precarious in the extreme. The narrative form is shared by all. This is the message resident in the ubiquity of narrative.

This point concerning the status of narrative is controversial at this time because of presuppositions common to structural linguistics in particular and to methods influenced by it in general. As one can see in the work of Ferdinand de Saussure, a basic strategy in methods of this kind is to treat a particular language as a closed system.[2] The components of that system are treated in relation to one another, particularly by principles of differentiation, of contraries. This strategy isolates languages not only from one another but from any possible shared ground. Referentiality becomes a wholly internal matter; language becomes a cultural container; and the gap between languages and cultures becomes impassable. True, some scholars who can be associated with structural interests and methods, such as Tzvetan Todorov and A. J. Greimas, press, as we shall see, for a general theory of narrative, one not restricted to particular languages, but this dissonance among structuralist interests between a theory of language that isolates cultures from one another and theories that treat the narratives of differing languages and cultures together constitutes more an anomaly than a serious challenge to the assumption concerning the relative standings of languages and the narrative form that structural methods appear unable to avoid.

Second, a reassessment of the status of narrative means treating it as a primary and not as a derivative form. Narrative produces and is not first of all itself a product. The British critic Barbara Hardy implies something like this when she says that narrative, while it appears (and is usually taken) to be an aesthetic invention, a product, is actually a primary act of mind that is transferred or lifted by artists from life to art.[3]

There are strong pressures on us to think of narrative as a product, as derivative. These pressures come from two contrary but mutually reinforcing epistemologies central to our culture: empiricism and idealism. The two, taken together, conspire to make the case that the basic, original situation is constituted by facts, by entities and events, on the one hand, and by ideas or beliefs, on the other. Dismissing for our purposes those who would insist on only the one side or the other, exclusive, that is, either in an empiricist or idealist epistemology, we are left with the possibility of acknowledging the claims of both, the value of both "cultures," to use C. P. Snow's term.[4] This creates very fertile ground for narrative theory, because narrative can be understood—and highly valued, one should add—as a medium able to unite these two original, separated components: entities or events and human ideas or beliefs about them. Indeed, imparted to narrative is an undeclared— perhaps unnoticed—soteriological function as a form of discourse that delivers human life from a condition of brokenness to a state of wholeness. Such a theory is recognizable in the important and influential book by Frank Kermode, *The Sense of an Ending.*[5]

Kermode describes fiction—for him all narratives are fictional— as the product of two contrary ingredients: meaningless, merely sequential moments or "now" points, on the one hand; and the mind's coherence-granting propensities, on the other. Kermode's sources for treating narrative as a product issuing from these contrary factors are clearly the empiricism and idealism mentioned above, for Kermode owes much to Hans Vaihinger. Vaihinger's declared purpose in his philosophy of "as if" is to combine Hume and Kant. While Kermode recommends a relentless skepticism on the part of critics, his interest is also to grant narrative a major role in human experience. Narratives, he argues, are always products, occasions of wholeness that need to be broken down into their constitutive, originally unrelated parts so that new fictive occasions can arise. Narratives provide the principal way in which a world divided against itself—that is, between facts and ideas—is always being made by human beings into a whole. The concord-making impulse is irrepressible and redeeming. Despite the emphasis in his work on the relations of fictions to the human condition within time, Kermode considers narrative more generally to be a product, to be derived, that is, from a situation constituted by two unrelated elements or forces: reality as it really is in its unordered state and the propensity of the mind and imagination for order.

Lest Kermode appear isolated in this understanding of narrative as a product of originally separated ingredients, we should recognize that his work reflects a general assumption or recurring theme in contemporary narrative theory. It appears whenever the narrative enterprise is presented as a product of the interaction between story material and the way in which that material is treated. Such is true of Seymour Chatman's *Story and Discourse,* as his title suggests, for an original gap is posited between the events or entities that constitute the material of the story and the way this material is treated, the discourse. One sees it in the narrative treatment of time in Gérard Genette's *Narrative Discourse* and Günther Müller's "Erzählzeit und erzählte Zeit." And it is detectable in the Russian formalist distinction between *fabula* and *sjuzhet* and wherever the influence of that distinction is felt in contemporary narrative theory.[6]

A corollary of the influence on narrative theories of these contrary but mutually reinforcing epistemologies is that the narrative world is divided against itself. A clear line, however difficult it may be to see at times, is drawn or assumed to exist between historical and fictional narrative. The one deals with facts and the other with ideas and beliefs. The legitimate need generally to distinguish between historical and fictional narratives becomes, under the influence of this epistemological situation, a declaration of a nonrelationship between them. Indeed, it is even thought that the criterion of truth can be applied only to the one, historical narratives, and not to the other. But as Paul Ricoeur has shown in his recent books on narrative, historical and fictional narratives actualize differing potentials within the narrative form.[7] Historical narratives are never without ingredients that are enlarged within fictional narrative, and fictional narrative is never wholly dissociated from experience. Nor is fictional narrative immune from the criterion of truth, although the kind of truth that it pursues or encompasses differs from the kind appropriate to historical narratives. The narrative form includes those kinds of narrative we distinguish as historical and fictional, and the form is not divided into two. Histories and fictions require and reveal one another.

The tendency to take narrative as a product of originally separate ingredients, facts and ideas or beliefs, seems to affect biblical scholarship as well. Two dominant interests are to be found: the reconstruction of the factual history of ancient Israel, early Judaism, Jesus, or the Church, on the one hand; and developmental or systematic treatments of the beliefs or theologies of the communities from which the narratives came, on the other. While this division of labor or interest is in itself not objectionable, the assumption from which it may come or to which it may lead—namely, that we have to do first of all with two originally separated ingredients, facts and beliefs, and that narratives are products of those ingredients—must be questioned. Such an assumption betrays the status of narrative.

I propose, in contrast to prevailing assumptions, that narrative, rather than a product of originally separated, non-narrative ingredients, is itself originating of those aspects of our world that we abstract from a narrative base and isolate from one another as facts and ideas. As Stephen Crites pointed out in his seminal essay on the status of narrative, there is no point so deep in the life of a culture that it is free from the narrative form, nothing prior to narrative upon which narratives depend.[8] The assumption of a prenarrative situation constituted of facts distinguished from ideas or beliefs is highly questionable. If we step aside from that assumption, we can consider that the distinction between facts and ideas results from the abstraction of the two from an originally unified situation, one that has an actual or potential narrative form. Nor need we take the narrative world as broken into two along the lines of this putative gap. True, in our culture we have assigned particular tasks to fictional and to historical narratives, and we are predisposed to read them in differing ways. But the separation between them is artificial or conventional, and it does not rest on an actual gap.

Third, reassessing the status of narrative requires a stress on its necessity. In addition to recognizing that narrative, because it is ubiquitous, undercuts the distances between languages and cultures and that because it is originating it allows us to distinguish facts and ideas from one another, we must recognize that narrative is not optional. The American novelist Reynolds Price testifies to this when he lists narrative, in the order of priorities for human life, second only to food and before love and shelter.[9] And psychologists such as Roy Schafer and James Hillman support the case when they describe how people whose stories have become too limited or have broken down completely cannot function and must be helped to live out of expanded or altered narrative situations.[10]

Generally we hold narrative to be optional, to be a matter of taste rather than of necessity. We may even disdain narrative as a form of discourse more suited for children than for adults or more for ancient and otherwise underdeveloped people than for the educated and sophisticated. As modern and enlightened adults we have the strength to view our world as it is without the illusions and comforts of narrative wholes. We have little patience for narrative and are tempted to press for an enumeration of facts or a set of clearly and sharply formulated ideas. This tendency within and around us to think of narrative as optional, even to be disdainful toward it, creates serious difficulties for a narrative theorist to be taken seriously in intellectual forums that are ruled by the separation of facts from ideas and the scientific and philosophical methods that depend on that separation. How can the case be made in such forums for an increased appreciation for the necessity of narrative when that case threatens the ongoing intellectual enterprise and its investments? The only way is by directly attacking the assumption that narrative is an infantile or primitive form of discourse and by insisting that scientific and philosophical enterprises proceed from a common narrative base.

While it may be relatively easy in a matter of a few pages to propose that the narrative form holds a status in and for human life that differs from what we often think it to be, it is quite another thing actually to acknowledge this status. Still more difficult is it to be oriented toward narrative as ubiquitous, primary, and necessary. Yet it is just such a reorientation that is needed. It would allow us to recognize that in and through narrative we have something in common with people who in other ways have little in common with us. It will keep us from subjugating narratives to interests in the history of peoples or in their ideas and beliefs. And it will allow us to recognize our own situation as always affected by narrative. The question, then, is not whether to take narratives seriously but, rather, how to take them seriously enough and with what consequences. It is in the context of such a question that a concept of scripture can and inevitably will be developed.

While it is true that the reassessment and reorientation called for here are difficult, it is also true that such changes depend simply on a recognition of a situation that actually pertains. If, as has been argued, we are in the world linguistically in a narrative form, then we need only acknowledge that. The ubiquity, primacy, and necessity of narrative do not depend on our wishing or giving it these traits. Nor is the status of narrative altered by our failures of recognition. That status will remain until the time of our inability or unwillingness to recognize it passes.

The Nature of Narrative

The second topic concerning narrative, its nature, is as difficult to address as is the status of narrative and as fraught with misconceptions. First of all, narrative, although immediately recognizable, is difficult to define. Hearers of stories attend to them without being conscious of how to distinguish narrative from other forms of discourse or of how to apprehend such discourse appropriately. It is not as though the hearer of narrative has a definition that is applied to discourse to see if and when it conforms. Indeed, since children are among the most ready hearers of story, the ability to recognize and attend appropriately to story seems unrelated, perhaps even inversely related, to sophistication and consciousness concerning definition. The immediate recognizability of narrative can fully be accounted for neither by contending that its nature is obvious nor by the gestures, tone of voice, formulaic beginnings, or other such signals the teller or writer may give. To the contrary, few people would find it possible to explain why narrative stands out as a particular kind of discourse, and were a person to begin with an immediately recognizable formula, such as "Once upon a time . . . ," and not follow it with a narrative, its absence would immediately be noticed. No commonly shared definition exists. While narratives are immediately recognizable, what makes them so is not.

The problem of defining is made more difficult by the fact that critics and theorists, determined as they are by particular philosophical interests, tend to underestimate narrative's complexity and variability. They limit their work to some, at times even to one, of the elements of narrative discourse rather than to all of them, and they tend to assume that one of the elements is always the most important one. By so doing they simplify the form and fix within it a center.

An interesting example of this tendency is the important study of this very topic by Robert Scholes and Robert Kellogg, *The Nature of Narrative.* They seem to deploy a quite complex understanding of the form, since they discuss three fundamental narrative elements: character, plot, and point of view. However, they soon begin to arrange these elements in an order of priority. Plot is given the lowest position because it is "the least variable" of the three. It is not clear why this mark of plot, if accurate to begin with, is detrimental to its importance, although lack of variability limits the possibilities of invention and artistry. In direct contrast to Aristotle, who took plot to be central to dramatic art, Scholes and Kellogg select "quality of mind" as "the soul of narrative."[11] "Quality of mind" is preferred to point of view because the latter has been attenuated in the modern period by the increasingly pluralistic and skeptical nature of Western culture. In addition, character is taken by them as the primary vehicle of meaning in a narrative.[12] In other words, while their definition appears to contain three elements, it is actually reduced to two: the relationships between characters, and the way in which they are described and depicted.

The reduction of the elements of narrative to two, the material (in the case of Scholes and Kellogg, character) and the way the material is handled, is typical of narratology. The reason lies in those influences, discussed in the previous section, that lead us to divide our worlds into two halves, material and the strategies for giving it coherence and significance. What is meant by the material may differ from one theorist to another. Kermode takes the material to be time rather than character, as do Paul Ricoeur, Günther Müller, and Gérard Genette. Narrative is broken down into these two parts, the material and what Scholes and Kellogg call "quality of mind," because of the dualistic epistemological situation that narrative theory reflects.

Another, more immediate source for the definition of narrative by means of two contrary elements is Russian formalism. The characteristic distinction between *fabula* and *sjuzhet,* between the material and the way the material is handled in the narrative, becomes pervasive in narratology.[13] This distinction is dictated not so much by narrative as by the epistemological situation, the separation of actualities from treatments of them. The definition is closely related to the derivative status of narrative described in the previous section.

The consequences for narrative of the critical and theoretical simplifications of the form are to curtail its particular kind of wholeness or completeness and to inflate its steadiness or centeredness. In the third chapter of this study, a variety of literary approaches to biblical narrative is displayed in order to reveal that each approach attaches itself to a particular element of narrative. The pluralism of critical methodology, in other words, is a reflection of the complexity of the narrative form and of the ability held by each of its several elements to dominate the whole.

Rather than constituted or always dominated by one or two

elements, the narrative form contains four, and not one of them is the "soul" of narrative, since any of the four can be the principal source of a particular narrative's force and meaning.[14] These four elements should be thought of as constituting a system. This understanding of a consistent system with varying dominants accounts for both the constancy and the instability of the narrative form. The four elements of narrative are character, plot, tone, and atmosphere.

The element of character contributes images of human life to a narrative, what Seymour Chatman calls "sets of human traits attached to a name."[15] It is the most familiar narrative element to modern readers because it is often dominant in the modern novel; the period, until very recently, has been preoccupied with individual existence, personal resourcefulness, or development, and the tensions between the person and society.

Plot gives rise to the temporal processes depicted in a narrative, to the image of time as coherent movement. In opposition to Scholes and Kellogg, who see plot as the "least variable element of narrative," we should recognize that plots can differ greatly from one another and that such differences are significant. This variety stems, for example, from the storehouse of plot patterns that constitutes the heritage of the culture's narrative tradition. In addition, a formal study of fictional plots will reveal three kinds of temporal patterns. One is rhythmic or cyclical; such plots, because they emphasize return, favor the past and are most easily expanded by natural metaphors. Other plots are patterned by the interaction of contemporary figures and forces. We can term such plots "polyphonic," and we can anticipate that they will most easily be elaborated with social and political metaphors. The actualization of a particular person's or group's potential is a third kind of pattern. It is oriented toward the future and is most easily associated with psychological implications. To continue the musical terminology, we can call such plots "melodic." While all three patterns may appear in a single narrative, one of them will be more inclusive and important in a narrative than the other two.[16]

While I shall be using the terms character and plot largely in familiar ways, the other two elements, tone and atmosphere, need new or expanded definitions. "Tone," a more precise and complex term than it is generally taken to be, refers to the teller in the tale, the implied or created author. This element has three components: material selection, voice, and an attitude toward the material. The teller relates something, does so in a certain style, and reveals a position in relation to the material. The last of these, the teller's attitude, is also complex, for it has both a physical and an evaluational aspect, both point of view and judgment. Tone secures the fact that all narratives are somebody's or some people's. All carry, in this sense, a personal stamp, although, as with journalistic reporting, that stamp may become very faint.

Atmosphere is the element that establishes the boundaries enclosing the narrative's world. These limits are secured by the sense of what might be expected to occur, of what is and what is not possible. In one narrative people fly and animals speak; in another they cannot. In addition to determining the boundaries of what is possible, atmosphere establishes the conditions affecting the narrative world, whether negatively or positively. Atmosphere is, therefore, tied to "setting," but it is a more inclusive and more precise term than setting. The time and place of a narrative go a long way toward establishing boundaries and conditions, but two narratives can have similar settings and markedly dissimilar atmospheres. "Atmosphere" is an element of narrative largely neglected by narrative theory. Seymour Chatman says, for example, "setting is practically terra incognita; my brief pages hardly do justice to the subject, particularly its relation to that vague notion called 'atmosphere.' "[17]

Taking the four elements together, a definition of the narrative form appears. Narrative draws attention to four kinds of force or meaning in discourse: subjects (character) involved in processes (plot) under certain limits and conditions (atmosphere) and in relation to a teller (tone). Narrative as a form spreads out these four foci of discourse as ends in themselves, allowing them to generate force and meaning appropriate to each. Any one of the four is sufficiently complex and effective in force and meaning to dominate a particular narrative and to deform the other three toward itself.

The Function of Narrative

Moving from the fundamental status of narrative in and for human life and from the complex definition of the narrative form as a variable system, something about the function of narrative can be suggested. Here again a difficulty arises. The role and authority of other forms of discourse—legal, scientific, or philosophical—are more easily detected because of their precision and their openness to tests of consistency or verifiability. The functions of narrative are less precise, but it is not too much to say that the truths and events that grant a people unity, identity, and orientation are entrusted by one generation to another in narrative form. This is not only true in traditional or archaic societies. Americans today identify themselves with one or more of the major stories available to them: the formation of the colonies and the struggle for independence, the settling of the frontier, the immigration at the close of the nineteenth and beginning of the twentieth centuries, and the like. The functions performed by narrative are important for the individual person as well as for a society.

The question is why narrative performs such an important and fundamental function in and for human life. One answer has already been indicated: Narrative provides an underlying unity to human experience, so that fact and idea, event and word, reality and mind, are related before they are separated. As Alasdair MacIntyre put it, "In what does the unity of an individual life [one could add group or social life as well] consist? The answer is that its unity is the unity of a narrative embodied in a single life."[18] In addition, narrative, by virtue of the comprehensiveness granted by its elements, is inclusive of four major areas of human interest. Finally, narrative, as I shall say more fully later, brings to attention the presence of these four areas of interest in all discourse, since the elements of narrative are concentrated or enlarged characteristics to be found in discourse generally. But these observations can be carried a step further, and the examples of biblical narratives well indicate the direction to be taken.

The biblical narratives used as examples in the next chapter will reveal that each of the four elements of narrative becomes a locus of divine appearance. This appearance of God in narrative form exposes the potential of the form and neither distorts nor unnaturally burdens it. The reason why the appearance of God does not tax or distort the form is that each of the elements always and inevitably leads to matters that are mysterious, that is, both urgent and insoluble, significant and uncertain. Each element of narrative leads to a set of major, unanswerable questions, whether or not the author or the reader is conscious of this direction or of the beliefs those questions require as answers.

The appearance of God in narrative form, in other words, reveals that narrative, by virtue of the elements that constitute it, arouses to uncertainty or quiets with beliefs four areas of human concern. The function of narrative—to provide a person or a people with identity and orientation—rests on this process. The elements of narrative incorporate matters that are both crucial for human experience and finally unresolved. What is both urgent or unavoidable and uncertain and ungraspable is or becomes a mystery, and Rudolf Otto's definition of the sacred as that which is both fascinating and intimidating comes very close to this definition of mystery.[19] The narrative form, at the point of each of its constitutive elements, therefore is able to engage the sacred. A particular narrative addresses or reflects orientations toward and beliefs concerning mystery at four points. These four constitute or correspond to a structure of belief undergirding an ongoing human life, whether personal or communal. A human life, which has an identity and an orientation, rests on a structure of belief that formally matches the narrative form as a system of discourse with four elements. Narratives become, then, articulated belief structures that either reinforce the belief structure of the reader or challenge it. This function of narrative can be more fully clarified by indicating those mysteries to which each of the elements of narrative leads.

Atmosphere, as we saw, is that element of narrative that describes the boundaries and sets the conditions of the narrative world. It determines what is possible and what cannot be expected to occur. It establishes conditions that are either hostile to or supportive of human life. The boundaries of a narrative world can be either more inclusive or more restricted than what we take the limits of our own experience to be, and the conditions can be like or unlike what we generally believe to be the case in our world. Questions concerning the limits of human expectation and the conditions under which life must be lived lead to great uncertainty. What the limits of expectation are or ought to be and whether the conditions of human life are supportive of or hostile to human well-being are questions only beliefs can answer. Individuals and peoples cannot avoid beliefs concerning such matters, and it is not possible to resolve differences between beliefs by appeals to reason or experience. In fact, what is believed affects what will be taken as evidence and confirmation.

An analysis of the element of character reveals a similar situation. Whether human nature is mean or worthy, whether it is in a state of decline or ascent, whether or not it is transformable, whether it is principally individual or communal—such questions as these, fundamental and unavoidable as they are, cannot be answered with certainty. Yet nobody can deal with other people without, however implicitly, revealing assumptions and beliefs concerning these questions. Narrative, because it is constitutionally committed to the depiction of human life and behavior, constantly provides or challenges such assumptions and beliefs.

Plot addresses beliefs because it is meaningful movement. Differences in belief appear in evaluations of the processes in which we are involved. Are they, for example, destructive or beneficent? In one narrative, temporal movement is restorative, even redemptive. In another, characters are crushed relentlessly by events that are cruel and arbitrary. Narrative time implies and affects belief because it addresses the question of whether human temporality is to be trusted or defied.

Tone, because it arises from or addresses questions of value inherent to relationships, also always involves belief. All three of the aspects of tone—material selection, voice, and attitude toward the material—lead to questions of relationship and value that can be answered only by belief. Something is worthy of discourse; voice reveals the relation between material and speaker and speaker and hearer; and position and judgment arise from convictions and commitments revealed in the attitude of the teller toward the material. This net of axiological and relational matters is woven with beliefs.

Narrative, then, is an articulated belief structure. The questions raised by the elements of narrative cannot be avoided, and the answers that they receive in a particular narrative cannot be verified. These beliefs work together to form a structure. We can infer this from the fact that a narrative constituted of the four elements provides a whole, a world. In other words, the axiological matters to which tone leads, the ethical or anthropological questions that must be answered by character, the teleological aspects of plot, and the ontological implications of atmosphere grant the four corners, so to speak, of the narrative world and provide a certain wholeness in their organic, although often tension-filled, relation to one another.

God can readily appear in biblical narrative at any of the four points constituting the narrative structure, then, because each of the elements leads to matters that are both crucial to human life and yet also beyond human understanding and control. This condition of uncertainty and significance is fertile ground for hierophany, for the sacred. And the appearance of God in narrative form reveals not only something about God but also something about the narrative form, namely, its liminal position, its relation to mystery and the sacred. Human awareness is related to mysteries by means of narratives, whether the beliefs embedded in the narratives are conscious or not.

This analysis of the narrative form in terms of its elements, the beliefs to which they inevitably lead, and the mysteries to which these beliefs are responses goes far in helping us to understand why narrative is indispensable to human life. It presents a basis heretofore not available for entertaining proposals concerning the status of narrative that have been appearing with increasing frequency, proposals such as this: "Narrative is not the work of poets, dramatists, and novelists reflecting upon events which had no narrative order before one was imposed by the singer or the writer; narrative form is neither disguise nor decoration." "Stories are lived before they are told. . . ."[20] Narrative is so fundamental, I am saying, because the four elements of narrative relate to a set of human needs and concerns that must be answered before a life can go on. These answers establish an ordered human world. A person's or people's ongoing life rests on a structure of beliefs that narratives articulate, beliefs concerning the possibilities or conditions of life, the moral and spiritual constitution of human nature, the processes in which both individuals and societies are involved, and the relationships as well as the values by which a person or a people live. Without any one element, the structure is incomplete; together they suffice in granting us the world we need, the world presupposed by ongoing lives. The structure of belief that narratives articulate or reflect is a structure presupposed by and indispensable to any ongoing human life. The form of narrative and the structure of beliefs implied in and by an ongoing human life therefore require one another. Narratives are, consequently, indispensable because they arise from or address the belief structure of an individual or a community's life, and, conversely, that structure of coherence has narrative potential, even, perhaps, an incipient narrative form.

The function of narrative must in one further way be clarified. To be direct: Narrative plays a liminal or mediating position between ordinary discourse and mystery. That is, the elements of narrative are to be related to the formal characteristics of ordinary discourse, but in narrative they are spread out, given special attention, and even granted a relative autonomy. All discourse deals with subjects (character) and events and actions (plot), even though, as in forms of the verb *to be,* the event or action is completed. Furthermore, every instance of human discourse has certain boundaries or limits (some subjects and events are not expected to appear), which are often socially determined but are in general determined by the conditions of the discourse itself and enfolded within it (atmosphere). And all discourse, even official declarations that are impersonally crafted, belong to someone, some group, or some people. All discourse is affected by material selection, voice, and attitude toward the material (tone). The elements of narrative reflect characteristics of discourse that generally exist. But in narrative these characteristics are stretched out, given direct attention, and elaborated. As a result, those matters of mystery described above can be encountered. Narrative holds a liminal position, then, between language and mystery. The function of narrative is to stand between ordinary discourse and the sacred.

This relation of the narrative form to ordinary discourse also accounts for the narrative potential of ordinary discourse. As Roland Barthes puts it, narratives are built out of smaller narratives as discourse is built from sentences. Indeed, for Barthes a sentence is a very short narrative or narrative segment. "Structurally," he says, "narrative belongs with the sentence without ever being reducible to the sum of its sentences: a narrative is a large sentence, just as any declarative sentence is, in a certain way, the outline of a little narrative. The main categories of the verb (tenses, aspects, modes, persons) have their equivalent in narrative, except that they are expanded and transformed to match its size, and are equipped with signifiers of their own."[21] Alasdair MacIntyre describes conversation as having a narrative quality, and he takes "conversation, understood widely enough, [to be] the form of human transactions in general."[22] I would add that all discourse incorporates beliefs, but in our narratives we engage those beliefs more directly and fully. Narrative, then, stands between ordinary discourse and the structure of beliefs undergirding human life.

It is not possible to determine a temporal relation either between the structure of beliefs and narratives or between narratives and ordinary discourse; primacy can be given neither to the mediator nor to what is mediated. One cannot say that beliefs give rise to narratives or narratives to beliefs. Neither can one say that narratives are determined by, arise from, and support beliefs or that narratives grant, challenge, or change beliefs. Both situations are reciprocal. And it is not possible to grant some kind of priority either to narrative or to ordinary discourse. By proposing earlier that the status of narrative is fundamental, I did not intend to privilege it over ordinary discourse. That would be difficult to establish, even if one would want to do so, and I do not. Equally untenable would be attempts to give primacy to ordinary discourse. As Barbara Herrnstein Smith puts it, "Fictive discourse appears to be as universal as natural discourse and we may suppose it to be as ancient as language itself."[23] It is, I contend, because ordinary discourse allows itself to be revealed as a world, spreading itself out, as narrative, in the four directions I have described. It does so in order to address four unanswerable but needing-to-be-answered sets of questions, matters the settling of which are critical to an ongoing life and that cannot be settled with certainty and finality. Narrative, in other words, is the arena, the threshold, where our ordinary language, like Jacob at the Jabbok brook, wrestles with mystery and, rather than overcome it, receives both a wound and an identity or name.

From questions concerning narrative theory I turn now to more practical matters. In the next chapter, four biblical narratives will be examined. The purpose is to provide neither exhaustive analysis nor a fully developed interpretation of any of them but, rather, to use them to illustrate several matters central to this study. First, I shall try to make clearer two points discussed in the preceding theoretical sketch, namely, that narrative is a complex and varying form constituted by four elements, any one of which can become dominant for a particular narrative, and, second, that the elements of narrative, because they lead to urgent questions that cannot be answered—to mysteries, that is—serve to make narrative discourse a liminal form. In the third chapter I shall use these biblical examples to clarify the major literary methods that are presently employed in the criticism of biblical narratives, to account for the differences between them, for the methodological pluralism, and to disclose the limitations of those methods. In the fourth chapter, also of a more practical nature, I shall use the critical methods and the four biblical examples to reveal the relations that exist between narrative and textuality. This leads to the theoretical issue of textuality that will be taken up in Chapter 5.

2

The Appearance of God in Narrative Form

My principal contention, in these general analytic and interpretative comments on biblical narratives, is that the appearance of God in narrative reveals not only something about God but also something about the narrative form.[1] Biblical narratives, for one thing, reveal the complexity of the form, because all four of the elements of narrative become loci of divine appearance. In addition, it reveals that narrative stands on the border between the known and the unknown, the certain and the uncertain, the domesticated and the mysterious. To reveal these two characteristics of narrative, one element of narrative will be stressed in each example. The Exodus narrative will be analyzed in terms of the appearance of God in plot. Judges will be analyzed through the element of character as a locus of divine appearance. The role of atmosphere in Jonah will be described to show how God is revealed through this element. And in the Gospel According to Mark the narrative element of tone and its potential as a locus of divine appearance become the center of attention.

To all of these narratives something of a disservice is done when one element is selected for particular, even exclusive, attention. In each of them all of the elements of narrative play strong roles. Yet in each instance a case can be made for the preeminence of one.

Plot in Exodus

Neglecting character in Exodus should not be taken to imply that an arresting analysis of the narrative in terms of the figure of

Moses could not be done. Indeed, Moses is a striking figure, particularly because he is determined in his role by his awkward position between forces that oppose one another and because of his personal traits of impetuosity and sternness. Likewise, the atmosphere is striking because unusual events occur in the narrative, things not common in the reader's world. Atmosphere places the narrative on an ontological level above that of the reader. And the narrator's inclusiveness, especially the ability to render private conversations between Moses and Yahweh, places the tone in an important, even authoritative, position. But however intriguing these other elements may be, plot, as we shall see, deserves primary attention.

Before looking at plot in Exodus some of the general emphasis on time and action should be noted. The narrative is packed with events: the call of Moses from the burning bush, confrontations with Pharaoh, the plagues, the increasing pressure on Pharaoh, the release of the people, their preparations and flight, the pursuit, the parting of the sea, and the destruction of Pharaoh and his forces. These major events, along with many other occurrences in the narrative, constantly tie the reader to action. In addition, time is closely reckoned in the narrative. For example, we are told that the spoiling of the Nile lasts for seven days. Later, Moses is told to meet Pharaoh early in the morning and to tell him that on the next day swarms of flies will appear. Careful scheduling and punctuality mark the events. It could almost be said of every event that "The Lord fixed a time" (9:5); he sticks to his schedule. This concern for appointed times and this compactness of schedule contrast sharply with the time prior to the outset of the narrative. During a vague temporal expanse the people, apparently through divine neglect, have drifted into a hopeless situation, one determined by events under neither Yahweh's control nor their own. Temporal process is also emphasized in the narrative by the way in which Pharaoh is placed under increasing pressure by the plagues, by his deepening resistance, and by the rising stakes. Rather than a display of unrelated events, the plagues become a calculated process that brings obstinacy to fullness and finally breaks it, occasioning the release. Finally, the temporal setting of the narrative is noted carefully. The plagues occur during the ending of the old year, and the preparation for departure occurs during the first month of the new year (12:1–2), in the spring, that is, the time of the new year for ancient Israel.

The plot itself has three major characteristics. The first of these is its complexity. That is, events are related to one another not by one but by three patterns. One of these patterns is rhythmic or cyclical. In fact, the whole of the narrative, from the call of Moses to the crossing of the sea into safety, has this pattern because the narrative begins with the mountain and the wilderness, moves into Egypt, and returns to the wilderness and the mountain. In addition, an almost formulaic pattern of repetition structures the encounters between Moses and Pharaoh, the plagues themselves, and the responses of Pharaoh. Finally, the Passover celebration is established not as a single event but as an annual repetition (12:17).

Along with the rhythmic or cyclical pattern there is also a pattern of conflict and competition. This occurs from the outset, when Moses resists Yahweh's call, but it takes its fullest form, of course, in the conflict between Yahweh's powers and those of the gods of Egypt. At first Pharaoh retaliates by increasing the burdens on the people. Then his wise men and magicians are able to match the power displays of Yahweh blow for blow. But with the rousing of the gnats the Egyptian counterpoint turns into obstinate retention. Finally, Pharaoh responds to the departure by pursuing the people. This pattern of action and counteraction or response is ended with the destruction of Pharaoh in the sea.

In addition to the rhythmic pattern and the pattern of competition and conflict, there is a strongly forward-moving direction to events, a pattern that, if the others are rhythmic and polyphonic, could be called melodic. There is one intention and end, the delivery of the people from their miserable state, and all is subjected to that overriding goal. The delays and setbacks serve to put pressure on this goal-directedness. The sending of Moses, the accosting of Pharaoh, the pursuit by Pharaoh, and the crossing of the sea give to the plot a strongly forward thrust.

Along with this complexity, the plot reveals a second formal characteristic: the juxtaposition of divine description with action. Events are regularly preceded by a divine account of what will or should occur. Yahweh repeatedly appears in the narrative, and he narrates extensively. This structure of relation between the text of prediction and the occurrence of events creates a strong, direct tie between Yahweh's word and happenings, between purpose and events.

The final characteristic of the plot is that it effects an exchange.

This exchange concerns the separated and the joined. In the situation given at the beginning of the plot there is one kind of separation and one kind of interrelationship, while at the end this set of relationships has been reversed. In Egypt events and divine intention are separated; it appears that the increasingly severe conditions under which the people live in Egypt were not determined by Yahweh but simply occurred apart from design. By means of the close identity created by the plot between Yahweh's intentions and the events that occur, an exchange is created. The narrative exchanges a situation of separation between events and divine intention for a situation of unity between them.

A second, contrary exchange accompanies this one. In Egypt the people live in close proximity to, are even determined by, the Egyptians. At first guests of honor, the Hebrews, under a new Pharaoh, have become slaves and even victims of mass murder. While this change from favor to abuse has major consequences for the welfare of the people, it does not represent an exchange, because under both sets of conditions, favorable and unfavorable, their existence and identity are joined to the interests of the Egyptians. The plot effects exchange within this situation. From interrelation the people are moved to a state of separation. This process occurs gradually. At first the signs performed by Moses are duplicated by the representatives of Egyptian gods, and the initial plagues affect the Hebrews as much as they affect the Egyptians. But then events occur that the Egyptians cannot match, and, beginning with the fourth plague, the Hebrew people and their livestock are exempted (8:22–24 and 9:4). This process of distinction-making culminates in the spoiling of Egypt and the departure of the people. Accompanying the process are many other stresses on distinction-making in the narrative—profane and holy ground, circumcised and uncircumcised, leavened and unleavened, raw and cooked, first- and second-born, blemished and without blemish, slain and passed over, delivered and drowned, this side of the sea and that side— "That you may learn that the Lord makes a distinction between Egypt and Israel" (8:23 and 11:7).

The plot of the narrative, therefore, exchanges one kind of separation for another and one kind of interrelation for another. At the outset events and divine intention are separated, while Egyptians and Hebrews are interrelated. At the conclusion events and divine intention are interrelated, and the Egyptians and Hebrews are separated. This exchange grants the narrative a meaning that is both more general and more specific than at first may be obvious. At the explicit level, a reading of the narrative is a reliving of the dramatic operation whereby Yahweh rescued his people from the slavery of Egypt and gave them a new beginning and a new identity. No attempt need be made to wrest the plot from this obvious meaning. A second, more general meaning is implied, namely, the power of God to deliver his people or a person from situations of distress and enslavement whenever they should occur. But it may also be seen that these obvious meanings share place with yet another. The situations "from" and "to" can be specified as pervasive and recurring in human life. Periodically, it seems, perhaps even annually, human existence drifts into a situation of distress whereby events and their meaning, actions and their intentions, seem to break apart. At the same time, identity, whether with favorable or unfavorable results, is taken upon oneself from someone else and an alienation in identity results. Needed is a process by which this situation can be exchanged for its contrary, when event and meaning are joined and identity is established apart from other human influences. It is the possibility of this exchange that the plot of Exodus provides.

God is revealed in the plot, therefore, not merely as the one who, after a period of neglect, rescued his people. Nor is God only the one who delivers his people whenever they are distressed. He is revealed in the periodic, perhaps annual, re-creation of human existence and identity. The unity forged by the narrative between event and meaning and the granting of identity that transcends social determinations are recurring human needs, and the meeting of these needs and the divine appearance, we are led to believe, coincide. When this exchange occurs God is revealed because it depends on a set of events that those needing the exchange cannot themselves effect.

This appearance of God through the element of plot does not place unnatural burdens upon it, because plot is always implicated in the question of relationships between events and meaning. This question is always a mystery, always a source or object of uncertainty or belief. The function of narrative is clarified by Exodus, then, because it brings the reader to the boundaries, on the matter of time, at which it is never possible to trace to human decisions and ingenuities the processes of dissolution and re-creation that mark such exchanges in human experience.

Character in Judges

Turning from the Exodus narrative to Judges, we encounter a less dominant plot. The tales in this narrative (Judges 2–12) form an episodic structure, and the plot is almost wholly rhythmic. The narrative is a repeated sequence of wrongdoing by the people, a resulting distress, a cry for help, and deliverance by Yahweh through the actions or under the auspices of a designated individual. The atmosphere is also less striking than that of Exodus; the events and actions, while often unusual and extreme, are generally continuous with those possible within the reader's world. The tone is similar to that of Exodus, however, being inclusive of both human and divine words and actions.

Notice should be taken of how important character is for this narrative. The death of Joshua causes a situation in which the people regress from their relation to Yahweh and begin to worship other gods. This means that for the book as a whole Yahweh is present or available to the people primarily in and through the power and influence over them of authoritative or impressive individuals. When afflicted by raiders and plunderers, the people try to fight back, but without the help of a leader they fail (2:15). When there is a human embodiment of divine power in the land the people are safe from their enemies, but as soon as he or she dies they revert to their chaotic ways and are afflicted by other peoples. The welfare of the people, their keeping the covenant, their safety from alien forces, and their relation to Yahweh all hinge upon the presence of a person. This situation is an explicit elaboration of the formal situation in the narrative: the dominance of character.

The embedded narratives of particular judges reveal an interplay between constancy and variety. That is, the positioning and the career of the judge have a certain fixed pattern, but within this uniformity there is great variation. Indeed, the name of the game seems to be introducing the greatest possible variations and offenses to the pattern without going outside the bounds of it altogether.

The pattern is announced separately (2:18–20), and it is embodied in the first judge, Othniel (3:7–12). The people drift into religious infidelity; they are given over to the domination or harassment of some neighboring people; they cry out in their distress; Yahweh hears them and calls a judge; the judge delivers them;

peace remains in the land as long as the judge lives. When he dies the pattern is repeated. Othniel's career follows this pattern exactly; from then on we have wide variation.

The purpose or consequence of the variation is to distinguish the judges as human individuals both from the pattern and from one another. If there were no variations, characters in the narrative would be determined by the cyclical plot pattern. They would be absorbed by the repetition rather than stand out from it and would, consequently, all look alike. In other words, character depiction and variance from pattern are closely interrelated. The people's behavior, its results, and Yahweh's response to the situation are routinized. The judges stand out from this predictability as distinct and largely unpredictable individuals.

The game begins with the career of Ehud. Little of his call is given to us, but the particulars of his treacherous act, of the victim and of the circumstances, are detailed. Not only do we learn that Ehud is left-handed and not only are we told, step by step, how the fat king is murdered, but the narrative's pace is slowed by the introduction of dialogue. Such slowing is inevitable with dialogue because the narrative corresponds in time to the time it would take for the event of conversation to transpire. Dialogue counters summary and ellipsis. A final feature of the narrative is its humor, which depends on specific details: the deception by a left-handed man, the large body of Eglon able to absorb the sword, the stench and the mistaken interpretation given it by Eglon's servants, and Ehud's escape while the servants wait for Eglon to finish relieving himself. After the individual exploits, a more general campaign occurs, and the story falls back into pattern.

The next story, of Shamgar, who killed six hundred Philistines with an ox-goad, introduces what could be called the summary judges. They have a two-fold function. First, they either offend or conform to the pattern. Shamgar offends it; there is no public infidelity, no account of oppression, no call and delivery, and no ensuing peace. Second, the summary judges lend a sense of extension and detail to the larger tales by virtue of their brevity. In contrast to them, the other tales appear lengthier than they otherwise would. Finally, it should be noted that Shamgar's position is appropriate here because his decisive act is, as in the preceding and succeeding stories, an act of individual violence.

The story of Deborah should be seen in relation both to the paradigm and to the Ehud story. The opening conforms to the pattern: the evil of the people, their being given over to the enemy, and their outcry. But two variations occur: The judge is on the scene before she is needed, and, later in the tale, the act of treachery that leads to delivery is performed not by the judge but by Jael.

The contrast with the Ehud story can be put in cultural terms. While, as with the Ehud story, the story of Jael depicts deception and violence, it differs by stressing feminine rather than masculine characteristics. This is clear not only in the prominence given to women here and to men in the Ehud story but also in the manner of the treachery. Jael uses hospitality and the offer of nurture. She invites Sisera into her tent. Ehud, in contrast, goes up to Eglon and thrusts the sword into him. In addition to the penetrations of the dagger, we have in the Ehud story the scatological humor of the misleading stench.

If these three stories are taken together, they suggest that comparisons and contrasts are established not only between individual stories and the pattern but also between the stories themselves. In their individuality characters are distinguished both from the pattern and from one another.

The Gideon story makes clear another technique for establishing the individuality of characters against the background of the unvarying pattern of infidelity and temporary fidelity on the part of the people and of patience and temporary anger on the part of Yahweh. Specific parts of the pattern are extended and detailed. In the Gideon story the segments in the pattern of evil, subjugation, and outcry are extended by the appearance of a prophet who denounces the people (6:7–10). And the call or raising up of the judge is greatly elaborated: Yahweh's envoy has a long conversation with Gideon; signs are requested and provided; Gideon taxes Yahweh's patience while he may also be taxing the reader's (6:39–40). In addition, the delivery segment of the paradigm is elaborated: the long preparation for war, the testing, the overhearing of the dream, and the campaign itself. Finally, the return to evil is extended and complicated by the contribution to that process by the judge himself (8:27).

As the story of Deborah needed to be related both to the pattern and to the story of Ehud, so the story of Gideon should be compared to that of Abimelech, of which it is a mirror reflection. Rather than extend segments of the paradigm, as with Gideon, the story of Abimelech offends it. The judge is not called; he raises up himself, is self-serving, and kills undefended people. Abimelech dies shamefully, struck by a stone dropped on him by a woman. The offense to the pattern is here so egregious that it crosses the bounds of acceptability; Abimelech is a mock-judge. The similarity to the Gideon story rests with the matter of political power, a matter emphasized by the father-son relation between the two and the offer of kingship and dynasty to Gideon (8:22). In the Gideon story the invitation to political power comes from the people and is not issued by Gideon to himself. Abimelech, in contrast, is power hungry, and he seeks political privilege. As a result he is humiliated, while Gideon had been honored. The simple technique of contrast helps to set these two characters clearly before the reader. The question is why so much trouble has been taken to make this contrast. The reason, perhaps, is that these stories depict individuals who have or are given, due to circumstances and divine call, personal power to lead people and to overcome enemies. The question is the relation of this personal, occasional power to political, established power. These two stories deal with this difficult but unavoidable question. Self-sought political power is far less acceptable than that which results from the personal power that suits an occasion, is granted by Yahweh, and is recognized by the people.

The inclusion of summary judges at this point again emphasizes the length of the preceding set of stories. Little more than notice is taken of Tola and Jair. Nothing is said of their calls or campaigns. Yet a detail is attached to each, lest they become only names rather than characters: Tola is linked to a particular place, and Jair is tied to the number thirty.

The Jephthah narrative begins with an extension of the infidelity and outcry segments of the pattern. Dialogue is introduced between Yahweh and the people. When the people remove their foreign gods they are able to deliver themselves from their oppressors without a judge. Like Abimelech, then, Jephthah is not called to be a judge, although, unlike Abimelech, he is asked by the elders of Gilead to help in fighting the Ammonites.

The character of Jephthah stands out because of his impetuous nature. While no direct tie is made to his youth, this quality of rashness may be continuous with the harsh treatment he received as a youth in his home, driven out by his brothers and disinherited. His career becomes the striving for a legitimacy and responsibility not granted by his background. This would account for his rash vow to sacrifice the first creature he encounters on his return from victory over the Ammonites. He appears to be an overachiever both religiously and socially.

The extended story of the impetuous Jephthah is followed by the summary judges: Ibzan, who, like Jair, is linked to the number thirty; Elon; and Abdon, whose thirty nephews, like the sons of Jair, rode on ass colts. Such similarities between some of the summary judges suggest that their relation to one another and to the longer tales is deliberate and formal rather than random or chronological. The inclusion of summary judges here also prepares for the longest and most elaborate story, that of Samson, because Ibzan, Elon, and Abdon are, like Samson, judges without an emergency, without a major campaign. In the Samson story many characteristics of the other judges are gathered together: an unusual birth, individual exploits, deceptions and treacherous acts, social legitimacy, impetuosity, and individual might.

The Book of Judges, in other words, reveals the art of character depiction. The stories have individuality even while each contributes to the whole. The pattern announced in the overture is crucial to an appreciation of the characters, for they stand out from the uniform pattern by violating it. They thereby gain their individual distinctiveness.

Still, despite the freedom taken with the pattern, the sequence of segments within it remains the same. Evil, hardship, call, and delivery are maintained in order. Behind the widely diverse characters stands this unifying pattern. Constancy allows the personal circumstances, aptitudes, and personalities of the characters to vary widely and to stand out. Violent or tranquil, male or female, selfish or not, acting on their own or soliciting the help of others, the judges are, at varying times, inventive, sly, outrageous, illegitimate, rash, or ferocious. Yet, with this variance and individuality, they are all housed by a single pattern.

The particular effects of these stories would be greatly diminished if the contemporary reader assumed that for some (especially ancient) readers the exploits of these judges were uncontroversial. The treachery of an Ehud or a Jael could be taken, although mistakenly, as consistent with the mores of some early readers or hearers of these tales. Rather than a distance or difference between readers, between us, that is, and earlier readers who were cruder in their tastes and standards, a gap exists between the readers of any period and the world in which these individuals carry on as they do.

The reader stands at a distance from these stories by being not, as with the Book of Joshua, in an ontologically less potent world, but in a world tamer in personal behavior. In the Book of Joshua a time is depicted that is more marvelous than the reader's; amazing displays of divine power, things not to be expected in the world of the reader, are common. In Judges a different kind of distance or difference is suggested. The reader lives in a more domesticated time, a time when individuals do not stand out so clearly in their distinctiveness and unpredictability. In some sense the reader's world is above that of the world of Judges, more civilized and ordered. Yet it is also possible to say that the reader admires this other world. Brutal, even barbaric, it was a time when individuals could be distinguished from the crowd as they cannot in a more structured and constraining world. Rash, fierce, unreliable as they may be, these individuals stand out from the background in undomesticated and memorable individuality. Something has been lost in the process of increasing the order and regularity of social, political, and religious life. The reader engages the world of the judges as glad to be delivered from such crudeness but missing and admiring it just the same.

The religious meaning of Judges arises primarily from the effect of contrasting a consistent function of deliverer with a wide diversity of characters. While the characters are human, at times all too human, deliverance is divine. It takes many forms, depending on the changing circumstances, gifts, offices, and aptitudes of the characters. Indeed, taken together they seem a summation of personality types. Rather than force the individual judge into the pattern to fit a divinely invented mold or type, the character brings to the office his or her peculiar ways of doing things. The function is thereby adapted to the characters rather than the characters homogenized by the function. Indeed, it becomes difficult to say of what exactly the function or office of judge consists. The result is that great value is placed on individuality, on distinctiveness of character, and on variety in human life. The bestowal of divine call and purpose on them does not displace or dwarf either the human potential of the individual or that person's characteristic weaknesses. And the variety displayed by the judges themselves reveals the constancy of the divine gift of deliverance.

The use of character as a locus of divine appearance reveals something about narrative at this, the second, of its constitutive elements. The element of character always leads to the mystery of human nature and power. The origins of personal power, of creativity, of forceful and decisive action, and of attracting and leading other people are a puzzling and fascinating matter. The variety and individuality of human nature along with a measure of continuity and similarity between people, the question of their basic trustworthiness and possibilities for transformation, are also all matters that bring us to the boundary of our competence and to the uncertainties concerning human nature that lie beyond our grasp. The mystery of character easily becomes the locus of divine appearance. Indeed, such appearance reminds us of the nature of the element of character and of the consequences of character for the function of narrative as a liminal form.

Atmosphere in Jonah

While atmosphere deserves chief attention in the narrative of Jonah, the other elements are also well developed and merit comment. The plot, for example, is readily noticeable, even quite memorable. The call, the flight, interception by and delivery from the great fish, success in Nineveh, and delight and distress concerning the shade bush—the plot offers a series of related incidents bound to engage the reader's interest. The events, as in Exodus, are tied not only by cause and effect but also by command and response. However, this form of connection is complicated by Jonah's disapproval of Yahweh's intention and by Yahweh's disapproval of Jonah's response. This complication turns the forward-moving, end-directed pattern created by cause-effect and command-response into a cyclical one. For example, at the beginning of chapter 3, midway in the story, we are no further along than we were at the beginning of the story, and the opening words of chapters 1 and 3 are virtually identical. The first two chapters, therefore, are a detour from the main line of divine intention and human execution. Half of the book is given over to detour. In other words, as much attention is given to the dissonant relation between intention and act as is given to their coincidence.

Closer inspection of the plot reveals further modifications of its forward movement. It is constituted of four separable units. The chapters as they now appear quite accurately designate these parts. The evasion of the command in the first two chapters is similar to chapter four, where dissonance between God's intention and Jonah's response also appears. The three chapters, 1, 2, and 4, have a retrieving movement, a going aside and even backwards from the main line of movement in order to rescue the reluctant agent. Chapters 2 and 3 are alike in that they both depict a delivery, that of Jonah and that of the Ninevites, and the action in both cases includes repentance and avoidance of destruction. In addition, a nice exchange is made in these two middle chapters between destroyer and rescued. Jonah's rescue is highly unusual not so much because of the physical problems of being kept alive inside the fish as because of the more spiritual status of a monster from the deep. This terrible creature is used by Yahweh as an occasion of preservation and delivery. Conversely, in chapter 3 that great military and cultural monster, Nineveh, is rescued from destruction by its repentance. Furthermore, the roles of agent and receiver are reversed when we move from chapter 3 to 4. In the first, the people of Nineveh receive the message from Jonah; in chapter 4 the Ninevites deliver Jonah from his self-centeredness by becoming examples of divine concern and grace.

In addition to a forceful and complicated plot, the narrative also gives us an arresting character. Jonah is impulsive, yet he is capable of reason and of defending his actions. It also turns out that his predictions of the result of preaching to Nineveh were correct. "This is why I made haste to flee to Tarshish; for I knew thou art a gracious God and merciful, slow to anger, and abounding in steadfast love and repentant of evil" (4:2). Jonah had desperately tried to keep God from the error of indiscriminate love, an error that, apparently, would subvert the meaning and the value of Jonah's own life. In addition to being both impetuous and accurate in his predictions, Jonah is both self-centered and self-sacrificing; although he sleeps during the storm at sea, unconcerned for the welfare of others, he is willing to be cast overboard when that seems the only way of saving the ship. Jonah is also capable of lofty and intense prayer, while not above the enjoyments of such comfort as shade in hot weather can provide. Furthermore, Jonah has size because of his many experiences. He has been down to the pit and up to the great city. Petty and magnanimous, active and passive, foolish and comprehending, Jonah is a man of many parts, a richly drawn character in a relatively brief narrative.

The tone of the narrative, as with all four examples, is notable because of its inclusiveness. It comprehends both the human and the divine perspectives, both the commands or intentions of Yahweh and the attitudes and responses of Jonah. This comprehensive stance of the narrator puts the reader in a peculiar position. Since the reader shares with the narrator the divine intention, the invitation is offered to disapprove of Jonah's responses to it. The reader is placed above Jonah, siding with the divine purpose and against the interest of Jonah in physical (sleep and shade bushes) and psychological (keeping Yahweh's love within bounds) comfort. The consequence of this position is likely to be disturbing to the reader, however, because the reader may share Jonah's desire to limit divine love more than Yahweh's interest in spreading it more widely. The price of standing above Jonah and of disapproving of his attitudes and actions, flattering as that position may be to the reader, is to lose the particular benefits to identity and orientation that a more limited divine favor bestows on those who are its objects. This position in which the narrator places the reader complicates the reader's relation both to Jonah and to Yahweh.

Consideration of the relation of Yahweh to Jonah leads to the question of atmosphere, the dominant element in the narrative, more exactly, to the conditions under which Jonah carries on or to which he responds. It is important to note that Yahweh, who determines those conditions, speaks at both the beginning and the ending of the narrative, providing thereby its frame or boundaries. The frame represents the conditions of human life as set and varied by divine intentions. Thus the boundaries of the story draw attention away from Jonah to the atmosphere that determines him and to which he responds.

The atmosphere that affects Jonah is largely negative. That is, the conditions of life generally counter what Jonah would like them to be. Jonah struggles with these conditions, tries to get out from under them, and tries to alter them; but they prevail. Furthermore, we should notice that the adverse conditions—the command, the storm at sea, the pit of the fish's stomach, the great city, the conversion of the Ninevites, the destruction of the shade plant by a worm, and the hot sun and sultry east wind—effect changes in Jonah's attitudes and behavior. The negative conditions, although contrary to Jonah's desires, are correctives. As a result of the contrary conditions, Jonah makes a confession of his faith, holds himself responsible for the sailors' plight, and allows himself to be thrown into the sea. In the constrictions of the fish he prays eloquently to Yahweh.

The great, alien city draws out of him his compelling and effective message, and its conversion evokes his remarkable confession. Yahweh's concluding lesson is occasioned by the loss of the shade. Adverse conditions, in other words, correct Jonah's course and enlarge his world. This means that the atmosphere of the narrative is only apparently negative; actually it is positive and beneficial. It places emphasis on a world beyond what is familiar to Jonah, the receding horizon of divine interests that lie on the other side of human expectations.

However, this extension of divine favor to the Ninevites does not mean that the particular is neglected. Rather than being preoccupied with the newly repentant Ninevites, Yahweh at the end returns to his messenger and deals with his distress. The deity's universal concerns in no way diminish divine relation to the particular, however petty and resentful Jonah in the meantime has become. The conditions under which human life is carried on in the narrative, then, play on an exchange or interdependence between adversity and benefit and between particular and general.

The inclusiveness of its atmosphere is supported by other aspects of the narrative. First, it is a richly intertextual tale. Identification of the principal character with Jonah ben Amittai of II Kings 14:23–27 ties the book to another anomalous period in the text of Israel's history. Ben Amittai was a faithful prophet during the reign of Jeroboam II. This period, evil from a prophetic and southern perspective, witnessed an exception from the general pattern of divinely sent adversity in times of public infidelity. Rather than suffering a loss of land, the people benefit from an extension of their borders. This prophet, who lived during a time of unmerited expansion of the people's life, now, in the Book of Jonah, is sent to Nineveh in order to expand the boundaries of divine favor. Second, there are references in the narrative to other liturgical material, especially to the Psalms in Jonah's prayer. Finally, there is a more general relation established by the narrative to the prophetic tradition. There are similarities between Jonah and that great northern prophet during the Omri dynasty, Elijah. The accounts of that prophet also have a narrative form, and they contain many marvelous events. Both Elijah and Jonah have powerful abilities for prayer; both experience fits of depression; and both go beyond the borders of their land.

It may, furthermore, not be too much to say that the Book of Jonah is grounded in the whole text of Israel's history. The God of whom it speaks is the one who creates all things and redeems the people: It is Yahweh "who made the sea and dry land" (1:9) and to whom "deliverance belongs" (2:9). The whole of Israel's experience of Yahweh seems summed up in Jonah's confession in 4:2. In addition, when Jonah identifies himself as a Hebrew, he reaches back to a designation used by Abraham (Gen. 14:13) and of the slaves in Egypt. Finally, his deliverance from the deep is reminiscent both of the Exodus and of the return from Exile.

Another indication of the narrative's inclusiveness is the way it combines the otherwise divergent religious interests of ancient Israel: priestly, prophetic, and sapiential. The references in the narrative to sacrifice, to the temple, to the psalter, and to repentance and cleansing all evoke a priestly orientation. The prophetic world is stressed, as already indicated, by the relation of Jonah to Elijah. There are also connections to the prophetic mode in the opening formula, the convention of refusal or hesitation, the prophetic distance from cities, especially among the northern prophets, the loneliness of the prophet, and his personal struggle with Yahweh. The sapiential perspective is represented by the emphasis on the cosmic order, the creation, the mystery of life in the sea, the storm and the mountains. The book also stresses wisdom in the *a fortiori* argument with its appeal to experience that forms the conclusion.

This textual inclusiveness augments that which the atmosphere of the narrative creates. The story goes back into the history of Israel in order to gather it up for a forward movement toward a broader future. The conditions under which Jonah lives are beyond his control. They generally confront him as contrary to his best interests. But they counter his desires not in order to vex him but to lead him beyond the forms of the familiar into the larger world over which the creating and redeeming deity presides. But the atmosphere also poses without resolving an important dilemma concerning boundaries. Despite the fact that Jonah at times looks foolish, he appears to represent a legitimate human need. Identity depends on limits, on boundaries, on the particularity of horizon. Without such limits, human life is disoriented, and identity is lost. Particularity and human identity seem unavoidably tied. But Yahweh is revealed here as other than human in precisely this respect: He requires no limits. Atmosphere, or the question of limits or boundaries that is always embedded in it, reveals a mystery, an unresolved contrast between human life that requires limits and divine mercy that knows none.

The appearance of God in the element of atmosphere raises to attention the relation of this element to mystery. Atmosphere provides the conditions and the boundaries of the narrative world, and it leads inevitably to the borders of our certainty as to what those boundaries and conditions are. We are unable clearly to say what is and what is not possible, and we are not certain if the conditions under which we live are ultimately favorable and supportive to our deepest needs and potentials or opposed to them. Not only does the appearance of God in the element of atmosphere fail to distort the narrative form; it also reminds us that whenever we deal with narrative we must deal with atmosphere, and that whenever we deal with atmosphere we confront the mysterious.

Tone in the Gospel According to Mark

With each of the narratives thus far described, note has been taken of the element of tone, although little more was said about this element beyond its inclusiveness, especially of both human and divine perspectives, words, and actions. This characteristic of biblical narrative, however, is no small matter. Tone, the presence of a teller in the tale, grants to biblical narrative a particular status and authority, for the teller within the narrative includes both the human and divine. Perhaps readers of biblical narratives are so accustomed to this point of view that they fail to notice its presence or consider its consequences. Indeed, "presence" is hardly the right word to use, since the narrator divulges neither identity nor the means by which access to the divine as well as the human has been gained. This position of the narrator can be illuminated, perhaps, by a comment the American comedian Bob Newhart made concerning the famous painting of George Washington crossing the Delaware River in a small boat. Newhart said that he always wondered about the person in the other boat who was painting the picture while crossing those choppy waters at the same time. We too should notice that there is in each of the biblical narratives a teller who is able to contain and to unify human and divine. We could easily wonder who this person is who knows what God says to people in private, who even knows at times how God feels about the human world that confronts him. But the identity of this know-it-all is held back. This concealment gives rise to all kinds of speculation and culminates, of course, in the religious or theological affirmation that the origin of the narratives, the source of the tone within them, that is, must be divine.

The choice of the Gospel According to Mark as an occasion to discuss tone may appear strange, considering the importance of the other elements for the narrative. There is a good bit of stress on atmosphere—the adverse conditions under which the ministry of Jesus is carried out. The plot, no less, has a major role; we move in the narrative from the beginnings of that ministry to its ending in and near Jerusalem. The element of character, the centrality of Jesus and the roles of the disciples and many minor characters, grants the narrative much of its particular force and significance. Despite the importance of the other elements for the narrative, however, it may be possible to say that they have their particular places in the narrative because of the tone.

First, notice should be taken of the point of view in the narrative. As David Rhoads and Donald Michie put it, the Gospel reveals "the unlimited knowledge of the omniscient narrator because no character has enough knowledge of other characters or events to be able to tell the whole story as the omniscient narrator has told it."[2] Norman R. Petersen presents a long list of moments in the Gospel when the narrator reveals more knowledge than any of the characters has.[3] Indeed, the narrator can even read minds and does so often enough to create the impression of always being party to privileged information but choosing to share such with the reader only at times. The narrator can depart from the story to report other events, such as the death of John the Baptist, or to anticipate the future, such as the betrayal of Jesus by Judas. The narrator can relate scenes in which Jesus is alone, scenes from which he is absent, such as Peter's denial, and the thoughts of characters that he would not himself know, such as Herod's opinion that John is a just man or Pilate's judgments on the motives of the high priest.

Another noticeable feature of the tone, along with the omniscient point of view, is the moral attitude it reveals toward the material. The way characters are introduced, as well as inserted views of their thoughts and motives, guides the reader's moral response toward the narrator's desired end.[4] This interest is enhanced by the narrator's divulgence at the outset of Jesus' identity as Son of God, so that the reader is in on the secret. By knowing more than the characters, the reader is in a position to judge them in relation to this hidden truth. This situation also creates irony in the narrative, such as when the reader is able to recognize the truth that characters, especially the opponents of Jesus, utter unwittingly or to observe how they misapprehend the authority of God in their attempts to make judgments on their own.[5]

The omniscient point of view and the divine authority granted to the judgment of people's responses to Jesus serve to place the reader above or ahead of the story at a vantage point from which to observe what is happening. This eschatological or apocalyptic place is a future state in which all has been completed and all made clear. The characters in the story continue, however, to be deprived of the benefits of that perspective. The results for the narrative of this extraordinary position of the narrator are two-fold. The first regards the narrator's relation to the reader. The second affects the other elements of the narrative, casting them in an eschatological mold.

By sharing the major secret of Jesus and his special role, the narrator places the reader in a position that exceeds that even of the disciples in the story. The reader is taken into the narrator's confidence and enjoys not only the position of viewing what occurs as though from above or from the end but also anticipating, by moving through the story, the position of full awareness that the narrator has occupied from the story's very beginning. The narrator is a gracious guide, eager to share privilege with the reader. The narrator also reveals a solicitude toward the reader that assures the reader that he or she is never forgotten. The narrator actually takes the time to address the reader directly, revealing a pastoral concern that the reader not be confused or feel left out of the storytelling process. The result is a remarkable combination in the tone of what we might call coolness and warmth: the elevation granted by the authoritative, eschatological perspective along with the rapport established by the teller with the reader.

The second result of the narrator's attitude is to grant the other elements of the narrative an eschatological dimension. The extraordinary result is the telling of a story in which a seamless unity is created between the momentary and the eternal, the terrestrial and the cosmic, the present and the time to come. We should look at each of the other elements of the narrative to see how this is achieved and how that achievement affects the narrative's meaning.

Setting is prominent in the narrative because Jesus travels so much. The Jordan River, the wilderness, the towns of Galilee, Gentile districts, the sea, along the way to Jerusalem, and finally the great city itself—the reader is always aware of where Jesus is.[6] Sometimes the locations are quite precise: the synagogue, a graveyard, someone's house. The narrator has not substituted some fabulous geography for the effect of actual locations, times and places. However, this familiar terrain is also seen from another perspective. It is the stage for an eschatological battle being waged between God and Satan. Satan himself, his representative spirits who control the lives of people, and the evidences of his evil presence— illnesses, blindness, and treacheries that victimize people or that they perpetrate—clearly indicate that the enemy of God is very much loose in this mundane world. The earthly setting becomes a stage, then, for confrontations between the greatest powers that exist. The narrator allows the reader to stand back and to view this larger setting and to be privy to direct confrontations that characters in the story apart from Jesus know very little if anything about. This is done with such regularity and ease that we may fail to notice the role of the narrator in creating this effect. The tone of the Gospel grants the teller inside information on confrontations between supernatural powers.

The depiction of such confrontations is complicated by the existence of another tension in the land: political domination by pagan powers and the resulting oppression of the Jews. The narrative would be greatly simplified if the two antagonistic pairs, God and Satan, on the one hand, and the Romans and the Jews, on the other, coincided to pit God and the Jews against Rome and Satan. But no such simplification occurs. The division between the evil and the good clarified in the conflict between God and Satan and, in the baptism in the Jordan River, drawing on a tradition of invasion of the land occupied by evil powers, does not translate into a contrast between two racially, nationally, or religiously identifiable groups. Rather, the distinction is between those who, regardless of their position or identity, recognize and support God's power and those who are blind to or oppose it.

The effect of the eschatologized tone on the setting of the story is to universalize its particularity. The atmosphere extends the horizon and reaches toward the final apocalyptic scene, the entering of the house of death in order to bind its power. Furthermore, it makes the particular setting of the story cosmically central. It suggests that what happens in this specific locality holds significance for all times and places.

The narrative's plot is also affected by the external, future position of the narrator. The pattern of action in the Gospel According to Mark is funnel-shaped. In the first, larger part of the narrative we are given, with a few asides in the action, episodes of Jesus' ministry in and around Galilee. These accounts have the effect of building tension not only because they depict Jesus as engaged with differing kinds of people, performing diverse acts, and addressing a variety of issues, but also because in these scenes knowledge of him increases while opposition on the part of religious authorities deepens. The pace of this section is very quick, as the action moves from place to place, and the size of the crowds increases rapidly. The pace slows remarkably as Jesus moves toward and approaches Jerusalem. His encounter on the way with blind Bartimaeus is presented in detail, with dialogue that retards the pace; the entry into the city is elaborately prepared for and executed; and a daily account is given of the stay in the city. The day of the crucifixion is carefully measured, and the process of his dying is detailed by the hour. Like a camera slowing the motion, this alteration in the pace of the narrative stresses the funnel-like plot and so places emphasis on the passion: entering Jerusalem, the encounters there, and the crucifixion. This move to Jerusalem as climactic is augmented by Jesus' predictions of his passion, by the "great multitude" that accompanies him, by the special entry, by the fascination the disciples reveal for the buildings of the city, and by the presence of the temple. Finally, the arrival in this religious and political center coincides with the celebration of the Passover. This fact allows the journey to Jerusalem to take on the qualities of a pilgrimage.

Because of the stress placed on Jerusalem by the culminating set of events there and by the slowed pace of the action, the pilgrimage to Jerusalem, the arrival, and the events in the city emerge as the culminating moments of the plot. Furthermore, there is a pervasive use of pilgrimage language in the narrative, a stress on the "way," on "going ahead" and "following." As Rhoads and Michie put it, "John is sent 'ahead' of Jesus and Jesus goes 'ahead' of the disciples. Jesus comes 'after' John, and the disciples 'follow after' Jesus."[7] This pilgrimage paradigm provides a convenient and effective directive to the action of the narrative. And Jerusalem is a place to which the characters of the narrative as well as its readers should go, both because of its role in Israel's history and because Jesus died there. But the move to Jerusalem is ambiguously portrayed. The city is also presented as unworthy of pilgrimage. Jesus finds the temple an unfit place, and, when the disciples try to increase his appreciation for the buildings that so impress them, Jesus responds by declaring that they will be thrown down. Most of all, of course, Jesus' mission is not recognized in Jerusalem but concealed. By going there, he exchanges life for death, acceptance for rejection, and large crowds for loneliness. As an object of pilgrimage, Jerusalem contradicts its role.

The strategies of the narrator, then, not only turn journey into pilgrimage; they also exchange the goal of pilgrimage. No longer need one go to Jerusalem, it seems. The reader is made aware that Jesus' pilgrimage subverted as much as it reinforced the religion of which Jerusalem was a focus. The center has been projected beyond the city. This means, consequently, that the reading of the narrative is a more valid pilgrimage than an actual journey to Jerusalem would be. For the narrative attempts to provide, as Jerusalem no longer can, a guide to the pattern of action created by obedience to God. And it reveals that Jesus made his pilgrimage to Jerusalem as much to subvert as to confirm its centrality.

The pilgrimage to Jerusalem has been exchanged, by this narrator, for the pilgrimage of one's life as a following of Jesus into death. Plot is eschatologized. The reader, like the disciples, should not so much follow Jesus to Jerusalem as emulate his willingness to become a servant, to deny himself and lose his life. The narrator of this gospel gives his readers a pilgrimage route that, while denoting a specific geographical path, becomes, by means of eschatological extension, available to all as a general pattern for life. Perhaps the narrator had specific reasons for creating this effect; the political turmoil and eventual destruction of Jerusalem in 70 c.e. rendered actual pilgrimage unavailable to many prospective readers. One intention of the Gospel may be to provide an alternative pilgrimage route, the narrative and the kind of life and death to which it points.

The consequences of the tone for depiction of character are similar. A gallery of vivid characters is presented in order to serve an eschatological end, while not slighting their particular and realistic potential. The apocalyptic perspective anticipates a final sorting, or judgment, to be carried out. This judgment reveals some surprises. Common people, many of them mentioned by name or described with what is, in light of the brevity of the narrative, elaborate detail, are preferred to the religious authorities. Pharisees and Sadducees are treated impersonally and presented as groups that oppose Jesus. The disciples stand somewhere between; they are treated both as a group, which often opposes the work of Jesus because his identity is not understood, and as individuals, singled out for particular responsibilities.

Of primary importance, of course, is the character of Jesus. The narrator presents him as two-sided: hidden and revealed, private and public, particular and universal, oriented to the past and to the future. Echoing or reinforcing this unifying perspective of the narrator is the position that Jesus himself takes as the narrator of parables. He stands outside the narratives in an eschatological position. His parables about the kingdom of God compare the present situation to a powerful, clarifying future. Crucial to an understanding of Jesus' stance as a teller in relation to his stories is the extended apocalyptic utterance of chapter 13. The future is displayed, from cosmic events to intimate, familial data, with a certainty that is normally reserved for describing the past. The only detail left uncertain is the date of the events. The narrator's relation to the Gospel as a whole and Jesus' position in relation to the stories he tells are, therefore, very similar.[8] Both speak from a later point where things have come to culmination, clarification, and certainty.

Jesus' position as narrator of the parables grants him an authoritative view of the world, a perspective unaffected by the transient and uncertain situation to which other people are limited.[9] If hearers recognize the authority with which Jesus speaks and the confrontational tone he adopts toward tradition and leaders, they do not perceive that he sees things eschatologically. The reader, however, can understand the perspective Jesus assumes in his parables and other forms of discourse because it is a perspective that the reader has been allowed to share with the narrator of the Gospel toward the narrative as a whole.

The Gospel's tone has, for these reasons, powerful rhetorical effects. The view of the whole places the reader in a privileged position from which to observe atmosphere, events, and characters. These secrets shared with the narrator lift the reader above the characters in the story. The crucial secret concerns Jesus himself. The reader is constantly aware, as characters in the story are not, of Jesus' special position in the divine plan. Not only does Jesus view things from the end point; he is also instrumental in establishing the beachhead necessary for the coming of God's kingdom. For this purpose he has a special relationship with God, secured at the outset by his baptism and witnessed to by his power over demons, his ability to do wonderful things, his transfiguration, and the testimonies concerning him in his suffering and death. The last of these range widely in quality, from "Hail, King of the Jews!" to "Truly this man was the Son of God!" Jesus is central to the story not only because he is present in most of the scenes, because his words and actions convey authority, and because he is the object of the narrator's interests, as the opening words make clear, but also because he embodies a meaning that provides the paradigmatic or configurational side of the narrative's structure. Somehow he has a special relationship with God, and the many things he says and does—especially revealed in the shift from the ministry in the north to his suffering and death in Jerusalem—obtain their meaning in God's purposes for his life. The scenes in which he appears have their importance both because of what Jesus says or does in them and because of that special, divine purpose. Lending greatest mystery to the narrative is the fact that this link between the life of Jesus and the divine plan is never specified. It is difficult to say how the two are entwined; the relationship seems to be present before the baptism, for there is no call and acceptance, as would be expected from the model of the judges or the prophets. And Jesus combines ordinary characteristics with those that derive from his special role. He is able both to calm the wind and to suffer fear, to exorcise demons and to face disappointment, frustration, loneliness, and physical pain.

Central to the religious orientation of nascent Christianity was the belief that the historical Jesus and the eschatological Lord were one and the same person. The writing of the Gospel is a way of affirming this unity. The principal way in which this proclamation is made is by the stress on presentness in the narrative, the effect of verisimilitude, coupled with the view granted from the eschatological or apocalyptic vantage point. This strategy is greatly enhanced by the portrayal of Jesus, the enigmatic figure who tells stories about and makes judgments from a similar position at the end of time. The role of the narrator and the character of Jesus are well suited to one another.

The meaning of Mark, then, is chiefly created by the tone, an omniscient viewpoint that permits the human reality and the divine investment to be held together. This literary possibility is the basis for and manifestation of early Christological interests. The narrator presents disparate realms as one, the mundane and the transcendent, the human and divine, the past and the future. No seam shows and no question is raised while the reading occurs as to how whole cloth is made of such incompatible materials.

The tone of the Gospel According to Mark presents a situation that shifts the question concerning the relation of the divine to the human in biblical narratives. It is not only that God comes into contact with human beings that is significant but that God, in these narratives, is comprehended by the tone, by an inclusive presence that encompasses both the human and the divine. What is this tone, who is this teller, able to do that? The mystery of biblical narrative, one could say, lies not only in the relationships between human beings and God but also with who or what makes that relationship possible. The answer lies in the tone, in the ability of a narrator to stand as far back from the material of the story as necessary in order to incorporate into a single whole ingredients so different or distinct from one another as are the human and the divine and to provide for these ingredients a common ground or meeting place.

The appearance of God in the tone of the Gospel According to Mark reminds us that tone always imbues narrative with mystery. Relationships between particulars and their value are established by tone, and events and persons are judged as to value or significance and distinguished from one another. The material selected, the attitude toward the material, and the language that creates a common ground between widely differing interests are all to be attributed to tone and are all matters interlaced with questions of value. The mystery of tone in the Gospel According to Mark, then, makes clear in a fourth way how and why narrative, as a liminal form, brings us to the borders of what we cannot fully establish, explain, or defend.

Summary

These quite general analytic and interpretive comments on four biblical narratives have been adequate, I hope, to clarify and illustrate three major points. The first is that biblical narratives vary formally because first one and then another of the elements of narrative assumes dominance. Biblical narrative, then, allows us to see the formal richness and unsteadiness of narrative as a form. Complexity and variability are exploited, rather than avoided. The second matter is that the presence of divine power, wisdom, or grace is revealed not in and through only one but in and through all four of the elements of narrative. In the Exodus narrative this power appears most fully in plot, the process by which one situation is exchanged for another, one set of relations and nonrelations for their contraries. In Judges the divine power to deliver the people is present in and through character, the personal force, resourcefulness, and unpredictability of individual persons. In Jonah the divine presence is primarily in the atmosphere, the negative conditions of Jonah's world and the inclusive housing of Yahweh's concern. And in the Gospel According to Mark the divine is revealed in the eschatological authority of tone by which the mundane and supernatural, the temporal and eternal, the past and the future are held together in a seamless whole. Finally, I hope that these examples clarify that the appearance of God in narrative form, rather than distorting it, actualizes its potential or reveals its position as liminal, as bordering on mystery. For the elements of narrative are always engaged in these ever unsettled but always needing to be settled questions concerning temporality, human nature, the conditions and boundaries of the human world, and the relations among and the value of entities and events.

3

Critical Methods and Biblical Narratives: Four Cases

A prominent feature of recent literary interest in biblical narratives is its diversity. Not only have well-known literary critics and theorists been engaged by biblical narratives; these scholars also represent the major methodological orientations that make literary studies today so rich or, perhaps, so confusing. An examination of the kinds of critical interests brought to bear on biblical narratives grants access to the forum of critical theory itself.

My purpose in addressing the pluralism of critical methods is not to offer exhaustive analyses of these methods or inclusive descriptions of all their practitioners. Nor is it my purpose to offer a complete survey of all possible critical methods and their permutations. I intend, rather, to discuss the major methods presently employed for the criticism of biblical narrative in order to draw attention to two matters.

The first concerns the causes for the pluralism; there are two. The more noticeable is the orientation of each method to some pre- or postnarrative interest. Each method carries to narrative assumptions or preoccupations, and biblical narratives are studied according to them. The second cause, to some degree resulting from the first, is that each method is more likely to attend to one of the elements of narrative than to the other three. The primacy of the particular element is fixed, predetermined by the method. Another way of putting this is that the diversity of critical method is determined by the complexity of the narrative form as well as by the theoretical commitments by which each method is shaped before it begins to address particular narratives. The relation of critical pluralism to the complexity of the narrative form removes the need for choosing one of these methods as superior to the rest. For while the critic of biblical narrative may not want to affirm all the theoretical assumptions behind any one method and may not be able to enclose those very differing assumptions in his or her own work, the methods can be used together because they also have, by virtue of the narrative form itself, a certain coherence. Indeed, since each method, as I shall argue, privileges one of the elements of narrative, it is particularly helpful in drawing attention to the force and meaning of that element. I shall try to illustrate this by applying the methods to the four biblical narratives discussed in the previous chapter.

Second, while I want to emphasize the richness that the diversity of methods brings to the study of biblical narrative as well as the important consequences, due to the concentration of interest taken by each method in one of narrative's elements, for an understanding of the elements of narrative, I also want to point out that each method is limited. Perhaps this is too gentle. It could be said that each method distorts the narrative form and denies its variability by implying that one of the elements of narrative is always dominant, always the principal source of a narrative's power and meaning. This is not only because the methods are committed, by the theory underlying each, to treat one of the elements as dominant but also because critical methodology tends to be self-confirming. This is because, as Rodolphe Gasché points out, method is a manifestation, in the main philosophical tradition, of the preoccupation with reflection itself, with self-reflection. This means that critical methods will not fashion themselves in response to narrative but will shape narrative to suit method. "Method," Gasché concludes, "is no longer simply the way to truth; it is truth itself."[1] My purpose, in these remarks, is not to dismiss a concern for method but to recognize that, while the fruits of critical methods can be enjoyed and employed, the complexity and variability of narrative, as revealed in the biblical examples, subvert the implicit claims of literary method to authority, even exclusiveness, and subject the methods to narrative rather than the narrative to method.

My procedure in treating the four methods, therefore, is to describe, first of all, the theoretical commitments that determine them. I shall then go on to say why each method is committed to one rather than to the other three of the elements of narrative. Then I shall discuss those aspects of the biblical narratives each method is particularly well suited to reveal.

Myth Criticism

I

"Myth criticism" designates a literary interest that relates narratives to recurring, conventional, or traditional patterns of human behavior. That is, agreement within this approach does not rest on some shared and specified definition of myth and its relation to literature but on the assumption that narratives depend upon a relatively limited number of recurring patterns and that such patterns are determinative for literature. A certain authority or primacy is assumed by or projected on the pattern because it is more universal than the particular narrative in which it appears. Such patterns also have the authority of age, for they are often designated by their places in the narratives of ancient peoples. Finally, universality and antiquity often conspire to grant the pattern a certain inevitability, a necessary relation to being human. Myth criticism is marked, therefore, by an attempt to relate literary works and criticism to such human sciences as psychology and anthropology.

A major contribution of myth criticism was to free literary analysis from the confinements of New Criticism, that form of literary study that was dominant in the 1940s and 1950s in the United States. New critics were oriented primarily to short forms, particularly to lyric poems, to the work itself apart from its larger cultural and literary setting, and to the relations within the work of words and their effects on one another. This orientation of the New Criticism made it unsuitable for long narratives, to which such close verbal scrutiny could not be readily given, and it cut literary studies off from the human sciences. Myth criticism opened literary studies to other intellectual disciplines as the New Criticism could not have done.[2]

Myth criticism is marked by a greater diversity of emphasis than is to be found in other methods considered here. This diversity is in part caused by the wide range of scholarly interests that affect it. Even within one of these interests, such as psychology, there are sharp differences to be noted between, say, Freudian and Jungian orientations. While both relate literature to recurring patterns of human behavior, the patterns themselves and what gives rise to them are points of difference between them. However, myth criticism is also diverse because its practitioners address not one but several of the moments in the aesthetic circle: the author, the reader, and those aspects of life that literature articulates or makes available.

Several factors contribute to the interest of myth critics in the author. One is the concern of many modern literary artists themselves in myth, traditional stories, and recurring patterns and figures: D. H. Lawrence, James Joyce, Robert Graves, T. S. Eliot, Ernest Hemingway, and William Faulkner, for example. Another reason for this interest in the author is the tradition, beginning with Coleridge, let us say, of distinguishing imagination as a faculty evidencing a characteristic form of thinking, a form that can be distinguished directly from scientific thinking by attributing to imaginative thinking a stress on wholeness and to scientific thinking a stress on distinction-making and division. A major spokesman for this contrast is the philosopher Ernst Cassirer. The distinction between mythic and scientific thinking is taken up into the work of many myth critics; one finds it to be basic, for example, to the criticism and literary theory of Philip Wheelwright.[3] Finally, attention is easily given by myth critics to the author because of the influence of Freud and Jung and their particular orientations to myth, Freud to Greek and biblical myths (Oedipus and Moses, for example) and Jung to recurring figures and patterns in comparative mythology, especially maternal figures and their dynamics.[4] These patterns provide ways not only of naming but of accounting for human behavior, and the presence of these patterns in works of literature draws attention to their role in the psyche of the author and in the creative process. While attention to the author is more to be noted in some myth critics than in others, all share an assumption that authors are to some degree determined in their work by the psychological or cultural influence upon them of certain recurring ways in which experience is ordered or interpreted.

Other myth critics are primarily concerned with the moment of reading or of the aesthetic reception of narrative. Philip Rahv, for example, writes that "one essential function of myth stressed by all writers is that in merging past and present it releases us from the flux of temporality, arresting change in the timeless, the permanent, the ever-recurrent conceived as 'sacred repetition.' "[5] Rahv is saying, in other words, that aspects of a literary work that derive from more general and ancient sources have an effect on the reader of a particular kind because recurring patterns eventually take to themselves a quality of timelessness and the transcendent. Reading a narrative, therefore, takes one from the world of the

contingent and changing into the world of the constant and enduring. This characteristic of reading narrative also allows the reader,
according to Norman Holland, to experience a kind of participation in the story that has distinct power and consequence.[6] He
refers to this level of response as "a re-experiencing of that earlier
sense of being merged into a larger matrix, a living forever in a
role laid down from time immemorial."[7] Finally, the orientation of
myth criticism to reception or response draws attention to the way
in which narratives allow the reader to move through the stages of
life. As a person advances in age, thresholds must be crossed—
puberty, vocation, marriage, parenthood, old age, and death.
Each threshold represents an exchange of one state for another.
Reading narratives can facilitate these transitions. As Joseph
Campbell puts it, "The purpose and actual effect of [myths and
rituals in traditional societies] was to conduct people across those
difficult thresholds of transformation that demand a change in
the patterns not only of conscious but also of unconscious life."[8]
Campbell interprets modern narratives as performing a similar
service for readers today, assisting them across the various thresholds or transitions that mark the advance of a person's life. This
interest in reading or in reception, while it distinguishes some
myth critics from others, is pervasive in this form of literary criticism. Assumed by it is a kind of relation created between patterns
in the narrative (which have greater universality or antiquity than
the narrative itself) and certain preconscious potentials within the
reader, something of a cultural or psychological nature of which
the reader is largely unaware.

Finally, some myth critics emphasize the relation of narrative to
its environment, to the world of which it speaks or which it helps to
establish. Following Emile Durkheim, for example, some critics,
such as Wallace Douglas, take literature to be a society's way of
establishing or challenging "basic social or class conventions and
values."[9] Literature, furthermore, can deal with that in experience
that is threatening or fascinating, even though a person cannot
address such matters directly in life—sexuality, particularly of an
unconventional kind, death, and unexpected or feared contingencies in life.[10] While this orientation is a particular emphasis of some
myth critics, it is generally true of this form of literary interest that
narratives are understood as dealing with matters of great moment
in life, either because of the authority of such moments or because
of their inscrutability and power.

II

After this sketch of the various orientations of myth critics and the kinds of scholarly interests that support them, attention now can be given to the more formal interests of this mode of narrative analysis. To what in narrative does myth criticism most easily and directly turn? The answer is that its principal point of access to narrative is through plot.

The preference for plot can be seen, for example, in the work of Joseph Campbell. His *Hero With a Thousand Faces,* a study of narratives from many traditions, ostensibly deals with character, as its title suggests. Actually, Campbell details a recurring pattern of events or actions that traces a cycle the hero follows: departure, the crossing of thresholds, and return.[11]

Perhaps a more exact statement can be made concerning the interest of myth criticism in plot. Plot has, among its several effects, the combination of movement and meaning. Paul Ricoeur calls these two aspects of plot "episodic" and "configurational."[12] The moving or episodic aspect tends to relate plot to specific and characteristic events and actions that give the narrative its own particular content. The configurational aspect grants these events and actions a certain coherence. This coherence has a more general status and application. So, for example, we have in *Moby Dick* the story of a young man who goes to sea and encounters new and unexpected things. But his many experiences could be said to constitute or be shaped by a traditional pattern of initiation. Myth criticism's interest in plot is especially in this configurational or patterning aspect. Northrop Frye implies this when he says that myths express the "universal in the event, the aspect of the event that makes it an example of the kind of thing that is always happening."[13] The configurational or mythic in plot is that which is inclusive, even universal, in its significance and is repeatable in its application.

Attention should be given to the work of Northrop Frye, whose recent book, *The Great Code: The Bible and Literature,* is an excellent example of myth-critical interests in biblical narrative. Frye's method is largely Aristotelian. This accounts, first of all, for his attempt to analyze and systematize the range of possibilities open to literature as a whole in a way similar to Aristotle's work with tragic drama in the *Poetics.* In addition, like Aristotle, Frye is primarily concerned with plot, for it is plot that grants literature its mythic qualities; myth is first of all plot, *mythos* as "plan" or "design." Going beyond the tragic plot, as Aristotle defined it, Frye ties all of the plots of literature together into one pattern, a seasonal cycle. He believes that it is possible to place the plot of any narrative somewhere on this cycle. Comic plots belong to the spring segment of the cycle, romance to the summer, tragedy to the fall segment, and irony to the winter. He elaborates his earlier formulation of this temporal cycle in a more spatial way when he says: "There are therefore four primary narrative movements in literature. These are, first, the descent from a higher world; second, the descent to a lower world; third, the ascent from a lower world; and, fourth, the ascent to a higher world. All stories in literature are complications of, or metaphorical deviations from, these four narrative radicals."[14] Whether he frames the patterns of movement temporally, as he does in the seasonal formulation, or spatially, as he does in this cosmic depiction, we can see Frye turn to plot as the clearest access to the mythic in literature and, therefore, as a narrative's central source of power and meaning.

When he turns his attention to biblical narrative Frye takes the whole of the Christian Bible to be a single narrative with a plot extending from the beginning of everything in Genesis to the ending or completion of everything in Revelation. He does not place this grandly inclusive plot on a cyclical grid, however, because it is linear.

The linear plot of biblical narrative is produced primarily, for Frye, by an ever-advancing movement of increased meaning and inclusiveness. The principal strategy by which this effect is produced is typology. Typology moves the biblical narrative forward in time because a type is always clarified or expanded by what comes later: "the type exists in the past and the antitype in the present, or the type exists in the present and the antitype in the future."[15] This movement from type to antitype grants a meaningful, forward direction to narrative time. The true meaning of an entity or an event will be disclosed in the future. As much as causality relates an event to the past, typology relates it to the future. Typology grants to the plot of the Christian Bible, then, a pattern by which the past is expanded by the present and both past and present by the future.

This temporal pattern also accounts for the relations between religions or cultures in the narrative. The narrative of ancient Israel's relation to Canaanite and other religions is one of taking up and superseding. That is, not all that is religiously different from the Yahwehism of ancient Israel is excluded; rather, much is included, but it is also reinterpreted. The values other religions possess are taken into, reconstituted, and superseded by the Yahwehism of ancient Israel. Its own religion made clear to the Israelites what other or former religions "really" meant. Frye proposes that this same attitude or relationship determines the Christian response to Judaism in the New Testament.

The third way in which Frye accounts for this cumulative, linear plot structure of the Christian Bible is by a pattern of increased inclusiveness. Although this pattern is not always consistent and clear, it still appears, he argues, as one moves from creation through law, prophecy, wisdom, and gospel to apocalypse.

The linear development of biblical time produced in these ways is complicated, Frye goes on to argue, by less dominant but still noticeable cyclical patterns. One of these, which is U-shaped, is a pattern of distress and deliverance.[16] In the patriarchal stories, Exodus, and Judges—indeed, throughout the whole of the unfolding drama—there is a repeated pattern of the need the people experience for deliverance from distress and of Yahweh's response to this need. While the causes of the need, the nature of the distress, and the form of delivery change, the pattern is constant. Another evidence of a cyclical pattern for Frye is the similarity between the state of affairs at the beginning, the Creation, and at the end, the Apocalypse. The completion of the plot in Revelation introduces an order of things that is more like the original creation than it is like any state between the two end points. This pattern of newness as restoration conspires with the U-shaped pattern of distress and delivery to complicate the linear biblical plot with cyclical patterns.

The interest of Frye in cyclical plot patterns suggests the work of Mircea Eliade, who, although neither a literary critic nor a biblical scholar, has enough real or potential influence on both areas to deserve comment here. Himself a novelist as well as a historian of religion, Eliade's work is calculated not only to clarify how people in traditional societies were related to their worlds by those narratives generally referred to as myths but also how modern readers can learn from ancient people how to cope with the problem of time.

Eliade describes the characteristic mark of traditional societies as their sense of connection with the time of creation. Societies regularly seek to overcome the temporal distance that threatens to separate them from the time of origins. Rituals permit withdrawal from the ordinary world and renewal of relation to original time. Basic to all myth and ritual are the abolition of ordinary time and the consequent return to the time of beginnings.[17]

For Eliade, every deliberate act in a traditional society has its corresponding narrative and invokes its paradigm from the time of the gods, heroes, or ancestors. Archetypal acts anticipate all possible human variations and applications. When characterized by return, a human act—building a house, for example—can become creative. Larger, more noticeable acts, such as initiatory rituals, the enthronement of a king, or a New Year's festival, are only more developed or communal forms of this same behavior. The whole fabric of human action in traditional societies is granted meaning by the narrative ante-structure that exchanges ordinary for sacred time.

The most important myths for ancient peoples, according to Eliade, are cosmogonic. These accounts are not forms of conjectural science but are the means for evoking a time that is responsible for the world's being a meaningful whole. By hearing the myths, people enter that time and emerge from the hearing reconstituted and refreshed.

We moderns, according to Eliade, fail to appreciate the myths of traditional societies because we erroneously confer reality and an independent value on historical or "profane" time. The consequence is that history, cut off from the time of creation, loses force and meaning. Nothing is more characteristic of our culture than its stress on linear time. Unfortunately, the human need for reincorporation with beginnings persists in this situation and brings about an alienation from time. And, "more strongly than in any of the other arts, we feel in literature a revolt against historical time, the desire to attain to other temporal rhythms than that in which we are condemned to live and work."[18] Fictional narratives, particularly, address today this human desire for a more unified, potent, and original world through that in them which is mythic, which is subject to repetition and reappropriation.

Two recent studies of myth and literature make clear this point of Eliade's concerning modern fiction. William Righter designates as mythic in fiction the aspect of plot that grants an order to events that is more, even other, than their sum. It is this order that grants a narrative its power. "The step is beyond history into structure, beyond the randomness of things into an order whose turbulent fragments are never stilled, yet which nevertheless enables us to envisage the totality which contains the movement, which in setting us beyond history sets us beyond time."[19] For Righter "the mythic" is the aspect of plot that grants order to the events of the narrative and relates that order to something in human life that is taken to be unchanging.

Eric Gould identifies this sense of the permanent and recurring within narrative as an aspect of language. He refers to myth as "*a response to the conditions of language itself.*"[20] What he means is the aspect of language that allows it to be a stable whole despite the fact that discourse is dynamic and variably to be interpreted. Along with the changing and the undetermined in discourse there is, simultaneously, stability and certainty. What in language grants these qualities is actually hidden, but it is to this that reference is made when critics, according to Gould, refer to the mythic in literature. Plots grant to narratives an interplay between the moving and the stable, the apparent and the hidden, or particulars and the whole.[21]

III

Having sketched the various interests that support myth criticism as a mode of narrative analysis and having indicated that within narrative to which myth criticism is mainly drawn, namely, plot, it is possible to return to Exodus and to ask what kinds of things myth criticism would lead one to say about this narrative. What else can be said about the order-granting pattern in the plot of Exodus?

With Joseph Campbell's work in mind, we can expect a myth critic to describe the plot of Exodus as a cycle. The hero departs from the familiar world of family and work; crosses a threshold into a threatening world, a threshold-crossing marked by the traumatic night with Zipporah; enters the world presided over by Mr. Holdfast, the Pharaoh; snatches the boon, the treasured people and the treasures of Egypt; and returns across the dangerous threshold of the sea, one that Pharaoh and his forces fail to negotiate successfully. Campbell would compare the pattern to that of many other stories. An example he might cite would be "Jack and the Beanstalk."

The interests of Campbell and other myth critics in psychological matters would lead them also to describe this journey as one that corresponds to the internal move from the conscious to the pre-

and unconscious world. The mountaintop on which Yahweh appears is a place of law and intention. The lower world of Egypt corresponds to powers of dissolution, darkness, and death that haunt the unconscious realm. These unconscious powers resist the development of an articulated identity, yet identity emerges from them, and they, when faced and contended with, make their contribution to the newly emerging forms.

Northrop Frye would place the plot of Exodus on the spring segment of the seasonal cycle. More exactly, its place on the cycle is from the unproductive, frozen state of winter, or ironic plots, and into the springtime of comedy. The people emerge from a long period of deathlike existence, from a place of oppression, to new, though uncertain, life. The actual temporal setting of the narrative, spring and the beginning of the new year, indicates this move of the plot from the end of winter to springtime.

Frye would also place the Exodus in the linear development of biblical narrative. He would stress that the calling of the people out of Egypt is an antitype to the calling of Abraham out of Ur. The difference is that this calling has greater meaning and is more inclusive. He would also note that the relation of Yahwehism to the religion of Egypt is not merely the relation of the true or real to the false or unreal. The Egyptian magicians have real power, and the Hebrews, as they leave Egypt, are not above taking with them Egyptian prizes. The meaning of this is the taking up of what is real and valuable into the life of the people, identifying the true nature of what has been taken up, and putting it to new and better uses. Finally, Frye would note how this linear development is complicated by the U-shaped pattern of distress and delivery, a pattern strongly present in the Exodus narrative.

The temporal setting of the narrative would evoke from Mircea Eliade comments concerning Exodus as a creation story. Crucial to such stories are the struggles of the creating deities with the forces of chaos, the defeat of the opposing powers, and the emergence of the created form. He would stress the cosmological associations of the story, especially in the plagues. Water, light, vegetable and animal life are all involved in these events. The ending of the old year is marked by the repeal or reversal of the cosmic order, and the plagues announce the ending of time as the creation of the new people announces its restoration. Eliade would find it important that the waters in the Song of Moses, as in Genesis 1, refer to the waters of chaos and that the narrative contains elaborate birth imagery: the doorways marked with blood, the death of the first-born, and the passage through water. Finally, Eliade would emphasize the formulaic repetitions in the narrative, the announcements of the plagues, their occurrence, the response of Pharaoh, and, most important, the celebration of the Passover as a spring and New Year festival.

Eliade's work on traditional narratives as creation myths also alerts the reader to the interplay in the narrative between sacred and profane time and central and peripheral space. The mountain where Yahweh reveals himself and to which the people make pilgrimage is a sacred place, and it is the center of the narrative. Egypt, because it is the locus of many of the narrative's events, appears to be the center, but it is really the periphery. It is from the center and to the periphery, from the sacred, to the profane, and then back to the sacred and center, that the plot moves. The role of the sacred/profane distinction is never forgotten in the narrative, and it accounts for the emphasis on acts of purification, divestment, and separation, of circumcision, Passover, and crossing through the waters.

Myth critics, in other words, would relate this narrative to other narratives that reveal a similar plot pattern. While it may offend readers of the Bible to have it suggested to them that Exodus resembles, for example, "Jack and the Beanstalk" or the New Year and creation myths of many archaic peoples, offense should not be taken. The effect of myth criticism need not be to reduce narratives to common denominators but to account for the continuing power and meaning of narrative in terms of the need for—and the ability of narrative to provide—recurring patterns of order and significance. For whatever other reasons the Exodus narrative has power and meaning, it also has them for reasons such as these.

Structural Analysis

I

The principal features of structural analysis are derived from the mode of scholarship from which it derives, structural linguistics.[22] This form of linguistics attempts to study language not historically, not as developmental, but as a synchronic whole. For Ferdinand de Saussure, whose work forms the wellspring of structuralist thought, language is a system in which particulars are recognized in relation to one another rather than in relation to their origins and mutations.[23] In language as a synchronically studied system, recognizability and intelligibility in language use are consequences of ways in which the units in the system differ from one another.

However much scholars may distance themselves from de Saussure's interests, they can be placed under the heading of "structuralist" if the principal purpose of their study is to infer from human discourse such implied systems. For structuralists linguistic behavior occurs within certain boundaries and conforms to tacit rules; attention to behavior becomes a means toward illuminating the units, relations among them, and the rules governing their use that make up the system. Systems can be "linguistic" in the restricted sense—constituted by words—or in a more inclusive sense, such as systems that govern dress or social manners.

Another emphasis of structuralism, one closely related to the first, is the gap that de Saussure introduced between a sign and what it signifies. This means, for example, that the relation of the sound "pencil," the signifier, to the concept "pencil," the signified, is arbitrary. The effect of this gap is to disconnect signs or words both from their conceptual associations and from their referents, so that they can be studied first of all in relation to other signs and words within the language system. While this move on the part of structuralists is controversial because it cuts language off from the complex of its relations to entities and events in the world, this move is crucial to the structuralist interest in the system of units itself. Structuralist modes of thought, therefore, lead more easily to the study of sign systems, to semiotics, than to the study of concepts and meaning, to semantics. This move on the part of structuralists also accounts for the highly formal, even abstract, nature of much of their work and for the frequent use made of algebraic and diagrammatic representations.

A third feature of structuralist thought, one that also affects structural analysis as a mode of narrative criticism, is the distinction made between language and speech, between *langue* and *parole*. *Langue* is the synchronic system of language, the sum of verbal signs upon which every use of language, every linguistic expression, depends. The primary principle of order in the system is one of binary opposition; that is, a unit has its place within the system primarily by differing from another or other units. For example, we distinguish the word "woman" not so much because we know what a woman is as because we know that the word differs from other words, from "man" or from "female animals." This principle applies to the process of distinguishing sounds, to phonetics, as well as to the meanings of words. In *parole,* in language use, a particular word is recognizable by its sound because it differs from other sounds, and the word has meaning by virtue of its difference from other words. Structural analysis, while it may begin with *parole,* with language use, is primarily concerned with *langue,* the system of differences and the rules by which those differences are distinguished and used.

The consequence of these three features of structuralist thought—that language is a synchronic social system, that the relation of signs is first of all to one another within a system, and that the system can finally be studied apart from discourse—is that the attention of structuralist critics is drawn away from the surface of literary discourse toward some system behind or under it that determines that surface manifestation. The meaning of any human expression depends on this background or code, which, although hidden, accounts for the import of individual messages. This system, moreover, is impersonal, since it was not at any time deliberately constructed, and it is determinative, since it establishes the limits and potentials in a particular mode of human discourse. What appears to be innovation in discourse is treated as an actualization of something latent in the system. Changes are accounted for by the rules of transformation within the system rather than by human intention. The system operates below the conscious level of a person or a society. Intention, particular discourses, and the conscious subject have a derivative position in relation to the system that determines discourse and social interactions.

In order to move from structuralist modes of thought to structural analysis as a kind of literary criticism, one must move from semiotics, the study of signs, to semantics, the study of concepts and meanings as forming a system. One must also move to a particular kind of discourse, such as narrative, a discourse that must also be taken in some way as dependent upon a system beneath or behind it.

At first it may seem that the structural analysis of narrative will resemble myth criticism closely, since both look behind the narrative to something more enduring and more general that determines it. Despite this similarity, however, the two approaches differ in several ways. First, narratives do not lead myth critics to a non-narrative system of formal relations but to a deeper narrative or pattern of events and actions. Myth critics primarily seek the story behind the stories, the myth behind the narrative, the inclusive meaning system that gives rise to its many partial expressions. But structuralists, even when, as with Claude Lévi-Strauss, they analyze myth, understand myth not to be a system that gives rise to surface meanings, not, that is, to be *langue,* but to be, however inclusive, a surface meaning, a language use, *parole.* Second, a myth critic tends to universalize meaning, while structuralists, if they universalize, do so in relation to form. That is, myth critics relate particular narratives to recurring patterns that express unchanging human needs, experiences, and aspirations. Structuralists treat language as conventional, as particular to a certain society, and as a closed system. If anything universal is implied in structuralist thought it is something formal, such as the principle of difference, of opposition, by which, it seems, the human mind operates and which determines the way in which language is appropriated.

Structural analysis turns away from the surface of a narrative and toward something behind it, then, not for reasons similar to those motivating myth critics but because of the distinction structuralist modes of thought always make between *parole,* a particular discourse, and *langue,* the system by which that discourse is governed. The move in this form of criticism from the surface of narrative to the system has been compared to that which a medical doctor makes from an ill patient to the illness of which this patient shows symptoms. The physician hypothesizes a certain illness based on the reading of particular, often unrelated symptoms, and the physician will then relate the symptoms to the illness and its properties as those have been abstracted and formulated by medical science. The patient's complaints are treated as symptoms (*parole*) of the disease (*langue*).[24]

The structural analysis of narrative, however, consistently faces the problem of defining and distinguishing *parole* from *langue.* What, in the analysis of narrative, should count as the *langue,* for example? Is it the particular narrative, with the *parole* being the various ways in which it can be interpreted? Or is the *langue* the corpus of the writer, the *parole* being the individual narrative? Or is the *langue* the narrative tradition of a particular culture against which the author's work is seen as *parole*? Or is the *langue* some general set of narrative possibilities inferred from an array of narratives against which any narrative appears as an instance of *parole?* Of these options, the last, the contrast between narrative as a system and a particular narrative as discourse, is the one most frequently chosen.[25]

The principal task for the structuralist analysis of narrative becomes isolating those components of narratives that appear constantly and that can then be taken as composing the narrative system that determines narrative discourse whenever it appears. The model for work of this kind is Vladimir Propp's study of the form of Russian folktales. Originally published in 1928, this work, since its translation into English in 1958, has become a primer for the structural analysis of narrative.

Propp identifies recurring units in a large group of folktales, units that he takes as constituting a system upon which individual tales draw. His basic insight is that components of one tale can, with little alteration, be transferred to another.[26] This observation permits the isolation of the units, which Propp calls "functions," in their roles as building blocks from which individual tales are constructed. Beneath the multiform and colorful display of the surface, of the tales themselves, there stands a remarkably limited number of uniform functions.

For Propp, these functions, while expressing action and requiring a certain sequential order, are static. He defines them by using nouns, for example. These functions are related, furthermore, not to actions or time but to the characters of a tale. A substantial portion of his study is devoted to delineating kinds of characters that appear in folktales and to discussing questions concerning their motivations. The interest in function, in other words, does not lead Propp first of all to a discussion of plot. The direction of Propp's work can be more clearly seen if contrasted with that of a theorist who moves from function to plot. Elder Olson, a theorist oriented primarily to plot, distinguishes function as primary in order to relegate character to a secondary status. He compares the writer to an employer who does not first hire a person and then look around for something that person can do but, rather, has a job to be done and looks around for someone fit to do it. So also the writer, according to Olson, is interested in characters for the sake of the plot.[27] In contrast, Propp emphasizes functions to turn attention not to plot and to movement but to characters and stability. Functions are emphasized not because they are more dynamic or temporal than characters but because they are more constant than are other aspects of character, such as motivations, attitudes, and names. Functions that imply sequence, such as departure and return, are presented as static pairs rather than as movement. Propp here evidences a characteristic move of structural analysis: developing a static system of components.

Structuralism is drawn to the characters of narratives because this kind of analysis tries to establish a system of units that is fixed. Characters stand out most clearly as units because they retain, throughout a narrative, a certain number of constant traits. Whenever a character appears in a narrative, the reader must be able to recognize it. This identifiability must continue even if the character undergoes major changes of situation, attitude, or even name. In his search for stability and simplicity behind the movement and variety of Russian folktales, Propp may prefer the term "function" to "character" because, in the material that he is analyzing, function is more stable than character. The folktale arises from a world in which social and economic functions remain relatively fixed, while people to fill them come and go. Hence, function becomes a way of talking more about the fixing of character than about the movement in narrative of plot.

II

The drift of Propp's work toward character gives rise to the hypothesis that structural analysis is primarily drawn to this element of narrative and most suited among the methods considered here for its analysis. This drift toward, even preference for, character can be seen in the work of other structural analysts of narrative. Roland Barthes provides a good example.

Barthes recognizes the difficulty of attempting to move from narratives to a system from which they are derived and by which they are determined, and he recognizes that such attempts are hypothetical. But, like Propp, he assumes that the components of a narrative are basically stable. Each sequence is itself a unit in a larger sequence.[28] This emphasis on units from which a narrative is constituted leads Barthes to stress character. He describes the first task of the structural analysis of narrative to be the classification of characters and their attributes. The second task is to classify the functions of characters, "what they do according to their narrative status, in their capacity as subject of an action that remains constant."[29] Only then should one move to a classification of action, to those units that can be organized sequentially.

This orientation of structural analysis toward the narrative element of character can be seen even more clearly in the work of A. J. Greimas. Greimas distinguishes three levels in the construction of a narrative. The first, the deep structure, defines the fundamental mode of existence of society and of an individual within it. It establishes the basic set of possibilities upon which discourse must draw and play, and it is, of the three levels, the one least vulnerable to change. The second level is that of the "superficial structures," the grammar of the signs that determines the manifest meaning of the narrative. The third level organizes the particular, manifest significances of the narrative. Of the three levels, Greimas is most concerned with the second, with the grammar of the "superficial structures" that determine a narrative.[30]

In order to establish the second-level grammar, Greimas grants to the determinants of narratives a stability and simplicity even greater than that found in Propp's work. As Fredric Jameson says, Greimas moves "to the level of semes [the smallest units of meaning] and semic interactions of a more properly synchronic or systematic type, in which narrative episodes are no longer privileged as such [as, Jameson thinks, they are in Propp], but play their part along with other kinds of semic transformations, inversions, exchanges and the like."[31] Greimas wants clearly to distinguish between "the narrative surface (or manifestations) and some underlying deep narrative structure."[32] He therefore reduces Propp's thirty-one functions to a six-part *actantial* model, which, while supported by his entire structural semantics, can be looked at separately. The *actants* underlying narratives correspond to semes in his semantic theory, to minimal and determining units of meaning.

What characterizes this model is its constancy and determining power. The surface of the narrative is an effect or a manifestation of it. The three levels correspond to three levels of human existence: the surface level to daily exchanges, the middle to the structure of a person's or a society's existence, and the deepest level to human nature, which sees the least change.[33] The *actantial* model exists at the middle level, the social structure.

The model places *actants* in complex sets of relationships, relationships that give rise to actions and interactions at the surface level. The relation of the *actant* "subject" to the *actant* "object" is central, and subject is related to object by desire. This basic structure determines that narratives at the surface level primarily concern the desire of someone for something. The object of desire, moreover, has a certain ideal or noological quality; that is, it is desired because it stands in a qualitative position above the subject. The object has this quality or value because of its source or because it embodies something that comes from some other source. The source of the desired object is the "sender" *actant.* The object of desire is sent to an intended receiver. The subject, therefore, enters and complicates a process of communication between the sender and receiver. Finally, by attempting to obtain the object, the subject becomes enmeshed in a conflict of forces that either aid or oppose the gaining of the object. These forces operate on the subject at the same evaluational level as that on which the subject exists. The model can be depicted like this:

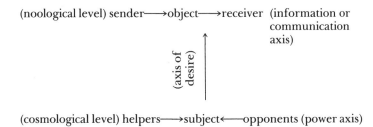

(noological level) sender——→object——→receiver (information or communication axis)

(axis of desire)

(cosmological level) helpers——→subject←——opponents (power axis)

These *actants* and their relations determine the characters of a narrative, the relations they hold to one another, and the ways in which they interact. Narrative discourse, then, is the manifestation of this underlying and unvarying model.[34]

III

A general description of the features of structural analysis and the particular example that Greimas provides lead to the question of what more can be said about character in the Book of Judges if this form of critical interest is employed. The specific characteristics of the book make it a good text for analysis of this kind.

Structural analysis stresses the system behind the various expressions or performances that arise from it. The Book of Judges indicates that something like such a system or, to use Noam Chomsky's word, a "repertoire" determines the process of storytelling.[35] In fact, a set of sequentially related units is given in the book: public infidelity, distress, cry for help, calling a deliverer, deliverance, and ensuing peace. While this pattern, since it is announced, lacks the kind of unconsciously determining status that structural analysts impute to *langue,* it does allow us to juxtapose a constant paradigm to a variety of stories and to understand the stories as a display of ways in which, within limits, the paradigm can be varied, extended, and offended. This distinction between the pattern and particular performances can be made in the Book of Judges, but it may occur in other biblical narratives as well. Such a hypothesis allows one to say, as does Robert C. Culley, that particular biblical narratives are performances based on some larger repertoire, the nature of which can be partially inferred from the narratives and then postulated. Culley, one of many structuralist critics of biblical narratives, uses the figure of a kaleidoscope to describe the process. Varying configurations can occur from a limited number of constant units. Biblical narratives as they appear may often represent only one particular shake of the kaleidoscope, so to speak.[36] The stories in Judges, then, can be taken to represent a series of shakes.

A number of rules may govern the particular performances in Judges. For example, there seems to be no prohibition against eliminating one or more of the units. In addition, units can be greatly elaborated and extended, as is the "calling" unit in the Gideon story. Also, it is possible to offend the paradigm so fully that the story becomes a negative or mirror image of the others, as with Abimelech. Finally, the units must appear in a certain sequence; although not all of the units need to be used, those that are used cannot violate the sequential order.

Structural analysis also stresses the study of particulars in relation to one another rather than in isolation or in relation to a world to which they refer. This principle may be applied to biblical narrative more generally, and its applicability to Judges appears particularly to be called for. The stories ask to be related to one another: the Ehud to the Jael story, for example, or the Gideon to the Abimelech. In addition, the summary judges may play a role in relation to the more extended stories, and they may also have some kind of relation to one another. When the stories are studied in relation to one another rather than separately or in relation to historical events, something about their nature in the whole of the book is clarified. Structural analysis may be able to reveal that the book has a kind of unity that underlies its surface variations.

It is also possible to apply the *actantial* model of Greimas to the Book of Judges. The stories fit quite well into it. They generally deal with the sending of a value to someone, namely, the sending by Yahweh of deliverance to Israel. And this gift or message of deliverance is pursued by the subject of the story, the judge. The judge, in desiring to attain the object, is assisted and opposed by surrounding forces. The formal *actants* of Greimas's model can then be replaced by the principal components of the stories.

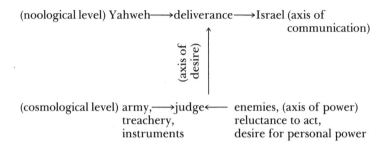

No claim needs to be made that this model can account for the principal figures and their relationships in all biblical narrative, but its usefulness as a tool to reveal continuities or constancies behind biblical narratives recommends it. It helps the interpreter to recognize that beneath the many characters of biblical narratives, as with any narratives, there is a more limited and stable structure of roles and interactions. The depiction of character in biblical narrative is often derived from an interplay, then, between a stable or standard role and the individuality of the character or the diversity of characters who play it. The two, the constancy and the diversity, are interdependent. It is because of the stability that the structure of functions provides that such liberty can be taken with idiosyncrasies and individuality in so much biblical characterization. The Book of Judges is a nice example of this interdependence.

The religious meaning of the Book of Judges is supported by this interdependence as well. A contrasting effect between the constant function of deliverer and the human, at times all too human, characteristics of the judge is achieved. The combination in the book of an unvarying divine intention and the varieties of ways in which that intention is carried out reveals that it is because of the constancy of divine purpose that people neither need all be the same nor slight or repress their individuality when called upon to do divinely mandated work.

Critical Hermeneutics

Hermeneutics, the study of problems in the interpretation of texts, plays a familiar role in biblical and theological studies. But recently the word and the interests it implies have entered the language of literary criticism and theory. E. D. Hirsch's *Validity in Interpretation* may be cited as a book that helped to make "hermeneutics" a common word in the forum of literary criticism.[37]

It is not at all clear, however, that hermeneutics is a form of literary criticism, although it provides a scholarly orientation from which a kind of literary criticism may now be emerging. In itself hermeneutics is somewhat abstract, distant from the problems of interpreting literary texts, since it deals with the nature of language and meaning, of the continuity and conflicts within and between cultures, and human temporality. In this regard, hermeneutics as an area of philosophical and cultural interest stands to a literary critical method in roughly the same way that structuralism, as a mode of inquiry, stands to structuralist methods of literary criticism. The difference between hermeneutics and structuralism is that the transition has been made from structural linguistics to a recognizable mode of literary criticism, while no such clear line from hermeneutics to literary analysis has been drawn.

One detects, in fact, a resistance to the idea that hermeneutics can support a literary critical method. For example, Richard E. Palmer, in his influential study of the hermeneutics of Schleiermacher, Dilthey, Heidegger, and Gadamer, argues that hermeneutics as a scholarly orientation opposes assumptions concerning texts that are common to any form of literary analysis. He concludes, "We must see the task of interpretation not primarily as analysis—for this immediately renders the text an object—but as 'understanding.' "[38] A resistance of this kind, one that identifies hermeneutics with an epistemology opposed to that assumed by literary criticism, joins other factors—such as the abstract nature of hermeneutical theory and the tendency of thinking that hermeneutics deals primarily with the problems of interpreting ancient texts—to retard the movement from hermeneutics as a general scholarly interest to hermeneutics as a form of literary criticism.

One step toward aiding this development is by modifying the sharp contrast that, in Palmer's statement, is established between analysis and interpretation. Another step is to specify particular tasks in the analysis of narratives that hermeneutical interests seem especially well adapted to address. Paul Ricoeur has already done this by turning his hermeneutical interests not only toward the analysis of symbol and metaphor but toward narrative as well, particularly toward narrative time. But it may be true that the most immediate relation of hermeneutical theory to the narrative form is of another nature. After these two steps toward relating hermeneutical theory to the analysis of narrative have been taken, the question then will be raised as to what critical hermeneutics would emphasize in an interpretation of the Book of Jonah.

I

The move from hermeneutics to literary analysis is facilitated by using the work of Hans-Georg Gadamer and Paul Ricoeur to describe the general scholarly orientation of hermeneutics. Both are interested in works of literary art as kinds of texts that most fully make available the problems of interpreting texts generally. That is, the literary for them is not eccentric but representative of language use and texts. This accounts for their strong interests in the literary, poetic, and aesthetic in language and experience.

There are several basic moves or assumptions that Gadamer and Ricoeur share. One could be called the decentering of meaning; that is, for both scholars meaning is interrelational, intertextual. Meaning, rather than identified with a particular form, is produced by interactions between differing, even conflicting, texts and the perspectives and values they contain. The result of this assumption is that the distances and differences between people, rather than producing barriers to meaning, actually allow meaning to arise. Meaning is the consequence of interaction between diverse interests.

This stress on meaning as the product of interaction places temporality at the very center of human identity. Rather than finished and stable, human identity is an ongoing, forward-directed process. A person or a people must trust this process if meaning is to arise. One must be willing to affirm the real or potential value of people who differ from, nay, even counter, one's own ideas. The process also requires a willingness to share one's own values and ideas with others.

The process of interaction by which meaning is produced has, for Gadamer and Ricoeur, three stages. The first has a negative quality; one becomes aware that another point of view challenges the adequacy of one's own. This stage may abort the process, because a person who feels threatened by difference may react to that threat by insisting on the invalidity of the other point of view. But if the process is not aborted by self-protection, a second stage is entered. One recognizes the contingent, limited standing of one's own point of view and the potential value of a view that differs from it. The value or potential validity in each is affirmed. The third stage in the process is the most difficult either to achieve or to understand. It would seem natural to propose for the next stage that some compromise be achieved between the opposing values. This would be the next step in economic and political occasions, where bargaining and negotiations between conflicting positions are a way of life. But a compromise between the two does not lead to the creation of meaning, since nothing really new arises. Rather than to compromise, the confrontation of conflicting values should lead, for Gadamer and Ricoeur, to the recognition of a broader human horizon of meaning by which both parties in the situation of contrariness are housed. That is, the recognition of values that differ opens up the possibility of entering a broader world than a compromise would provide. Suspending compromise or resolution between differences and affirming differing values lead to the affirmation of a broader horizon of potential meaning that is revealed as a future possibility by the process. It is to this horizon, this larger world, that the hermeneutical theories of Gadamer and Ricoeur are primarily pointed.

These shared characteristics of the thought of Gadamer and Ricoeur—that meaning is interrelational, that interrelational process implies the primacy and trustworthiness of temporality in human life, and that these processes have three stages—grant a general orientation to hermeneutical theory. The special emphases of Gadamer, first, and then of Ricoeur can now, however briefly, be discussed.

Three pivotal words in the work of Gadamer are "language," "experience," and "tradition." As to language, Gadamer stresses two matters: "Language" is always related to "world," and "language" is always changing. Unlike structuralists, then, Gadamer views language neither as abstracted from "world" nor as static. For him language and world are interdependent. To isolate one from the other, to oppose them as contraries, is possible only in abstraction. Language and world involve and require one another. "Not only is the world 'world' only insofar as it comes into language, but language, too, has its real being only in the fact that the world is represented within it."[39] Language is a "world," and "world" has linguistic properties. Furthermore, language and world are always changing. The principal cause for change is interaction between people and cultures. When people attempt to understand one another, the language and the world of each are simultaneously affected. Such interactions occur not only constantly but also at many levels, since every person lives in several linguistic worlds: individual, familial, social, cultural, and the linguistic world inclusive of all human languages, a world that allows German and English, for example, to alter one another, however slightly and gradually. Human identity, what it means to say "I," therefore, is inseparable from this constant, many-leveled interpenetration between language worlds in which a person participates and language worlds a person encounters as alien.[40]

The nature of experience is also a central matter for Gadamer, especially as it applies to aesthetic experience. We tend to think of experiences as individuated and detached. This is the consequence of empiricism, which construes experiences as isolated events. When this notion joins with the Kantian emphasis on the aesthetic as holding a status of its own, free from questions of truth, aesthetic experience becomes especially insulated and discrete. Gadamer argues, however, that when an experience stands out as particularly noticeable or meaningful, when we are aware of an experience, this is due not to its detachment from the rest of life but to its relevance to it. An experience stands out because it holds significance for a large measure of one's life. One's entire world may be involved in and affected by "an experience." "Every experience is taken out of the continuity of life and at the same time related to the whole of one's life."[41] It is particularly true of aesthetic experiences that they stand out, that one is aware of them, because they hold implications for the whole of one's world.

"Tradition" is the word Gadamer uses for the world that one brings to, or that is affected by, experience. He discusses the nature of tradition through the roles of "common sense" and "good taste." These cultural standards, when evoked, indicate participation in a tradition that has an immediately recognizable but not wholly articulated meaning. With an appeal to good taste or common sense, one summons the force and meaning of tradition. This tradition, according to Gadamer, is always changing. This is because tradition does not move in time but is itself temporal; that is, the passage of time is not a simple movement from one "now" to the next but is a process that always involves the interrelation and effect upon one another of past, present, and future. This means that for Gadamer events and experiences are related both to their causes and to their results. These results never come to an end. The world, then, is a constant, dynamic interplay between the meanings that are particularized in recognizable experiences and their causes and consequences.

These three terms—language, experience, and tradition—undergird Gadamer's discussion of what occurs when a person interprets a text. In a text one confronts not only language but a world and a tradition as well. Consequently, the process of interpretation does not depend on isolating the text. Nor does it attribute the text solely to the mind and intentions of its author. Gadamer opposes the hermeneutics of Schleiermacher, by which a text is interpreted by re-creating its origin—the author or the author's intention. He calls such hermeneutics "ultimately a divinatory process, a placing of oneself within the mind of the author . . . a recreation of the creative act."[42] For Gadamer the hermeneutical task is more complex. While there is surely always an author of the text, the text gives the author's world. Not only this—texts make available to the reader that which in the author's world is not limited to a particular place and time but is accessible to readers distant from them.

Complicating the problem of interpretation further is the fact that the reader does not stand as an isolated unit with a mind free of assumptions, needs, and expectations. Rather, the reader also represents a world. Reading, then, brings together two differing worlds. Interpretation is the process by which the differences between the world of the text and the world of the reader are treated. As a result of these interactions both text and reader are altered. The reader's world has been challenged and expanded by the text. The reading of the text, meanwhile, whether minimally or dramatically, affects the tradition in which that text stands. Future readings will be affected by this alteration made in the tradition and in the text's standing within it.

The interpretation of a work of art epitomizes this process. For example, it is particularly true of aesthetic texts—poems, let us say—that they present a world. Works of art are not simply functional, not simply limited to a particular place, time, and use. What makes a work of art powerful is its ability, while arising from a particular place and time, to make the reality of that time and place available to others distant from it. Art becomes art precisely not by being confined but by making available to people what in the particular is generally significant. Consequently, a reader can still be deeply affected by Sophoclean drama despite the great distance between the classical and modern worlds. Furthermore, interpreting a text of which one has an aesthetic experience means interpreting a text in the reading of which one's own world was implicated. The interpretation then becomes an articulation of the reasons for and the consequences of this coming together of the world of the text and the world of the reader. This coming together affects both. The reader's world is affected by the text, and the meaning of the text is affected by every response to it.

The principal, final hermeneutical task is not to draw attention to that in the text or that in the reader which gives rise to understanding between them but to draw attention to that ground or horizon that makes the interaction possible by housing or accommodating it. This third party is not so much behind or beneath the reader and the text as ahead of them. It is an only partially apprehendable horizon of larger significance that encompasses within it the worlds of text and reader, however different from one another those worlds may be. Interpretation, then, is never conclusive or completed. This is due, first of all, not to inscrutable ingredients in the text nor to preconscious resources in the mind of the reader but to the horizon itself as both an always retreating boundary of significance and as a significance that is not the product of conscious design.

Paul Ricoeur's work in hermeneutics arises from an exchange in his philosophical anthropology in ways of talking about human limitation. In *Fallible Man* he turns from more direct ways, derived from existentialism, to indirect ways derived from religious language. Instead of speaking of human limitations and finitude he turns to the more symbolic language of defilement, brokenness, and unworthiness. Such language cannot be interpreted directly. That is, one can speak rather directly of what it means to be limited; a person, for example, cannot be in two places at the same time. But one cannot speak so directly about the sense of being unworthy or unclean. This is symbolic language, requiring another kind of appropriation.[43]

Two aspects of Ricoeur's work with symbol should be mentioned. The first is his conclusion that symbols are stretched; that is, they have their power and meaning because they are able, by extension, to include something from both boundaries of the human world. These boundaries can be denoted in a number of ways—past and future, mundane and spiritual, internal and external. It is not so much *that* symbols have complex meanings and can be variously interpreted as it is *why* symbols have such complexity that interests Ricoeur. The reason arises from the temporality of discourse, from the way in which discourse always means more than one intends. This fact is perhaps most obvious in what are called "Freudian slips," unintended disclosures of significance. But it is always true, and not only at times of certain slips, that one reveals in discourse more of his or her self and world than one realizes and controls. Language, although used in the present, actually stretches backwards to reveal something about the speaker's past, bodily situation in the world, and internal dynamics. This is also true of the future, the spiritual and external limit toward which language use in the present is stretched. One can recognize this by the fact that something said now can have meaning in future situations as well as in the present; in fact, at times something said may have more significance later than at the time it was said. Discourse in the present stretches between, reveals something about, both the past and the future. In discourse one is always bringing one's past along and always anticipating the future.

Symbols, revealing the complex standing of discourse, must be interpreted accordingly. The Freudian direction, toward the past, the internal, and the carnal, Ricoeur calls archaeological hermeneutics. The forward, spiritual, and external (one could say Hegelian) direction he calls teleological hermeneutics. The first brings the interpreter to the borders between language and life, the second to the borders between language and spirit.[44]

A second aspect of Ricoeur's study of symbol is that he considers symbols as calling attention to a dimension or characteristic of all discourse. Discourse always means more than the present can exhaust or the speaker intends. It is also always making present a world that is past and anticipating a world yet to come. The polysemic nature of language is not only that words and discourses can have many meanings. It is also that language, as we use it, is constantly doing for us a work of which we are not fully aware; namely, it is keeping our past and future, our internality and externality, our bodies and our spirits from being divided from one another.

Symbols make us aware of this activity. So, for example, the symbol of defilement as an expression of human fallibility may strike us now as quite naive, since we tend not to think of guilt in terms of dirt on one's body; one is not told by a counselor to treat guilt by washing. Still, we are well aware of the force of this symbol, of the way in which the internal and external, the physical and the moral, are united in the symbols of defilement and washing. Ricoeur urges that we cannot do without such language. If a symbol, such as defilement, appears to us as hopelessly naive, we should recognize the importance of the work it is doing and anticipate some kind of language that will do the same. To strip language of its symbols and to repress the symbolic dimension of all language are both ultimately futile and a dangerous deprivation of the wholeness of the human world.[45]

These characteristics of his theory of symbols reveal how closely Ricoeur works with the nature of language and with temporality. This is also evident in his work with metaphor. Drawing on Aristotle, Ricoeur argues that the principal characteristic of metaphor is that it violates an already constituted order. This violation is a deconstructive intermediary phase between description and re-description. Metaphor subverts order or confuses categories in order to create or to adumbrate a new order. What metaphor noticeably accomplishes occurs in language constantly. Words are always being used in new sentences and new situations. Words carry the effects of these uses. Every sentence, however unnoticeably and minimally, alters the meaning of a word, both because it is part of a new discourse and because it is uttered or written in a new situation. Metaphor brings to attention a dimension or consequence of discourse that is always occurring.

Metaphors result, then, from an impasse between the lexical possibilities of a word and the inapplicability of those possibilities to a particular sentence. This impasse is transcended by the release of a new meaning that rescues the sentence from meaninglessness. Metaphor forces the sentence, then, to jump tracks, to uncover a new pertinence despite the impertinence, the calculated or unconscious error. The word is affected by the new meaning.[46]

Ricoeur's treatment of metaphor, as with symbol, reveals how language both creates and unifies our world. Recognizable metaphors make clear what is constantly going on in language. The given lexical meaning of words—that is, what they have meant in the past—is always being violated or subverted by their uses in the new situation. This means that our worlds are not fixed by lexical meanings but that a dynamic interrelationship is carried on through language use between order and subversion, past and future, familiar and new. Metaphor alerts us to the fact that when we interpret discourse we are attentive to at least two things: what a word means (its lexical order) and what it means in this sentence (its predicative order).[47] By virtue of its metaphoric dimension, language not only submits to innovation; it often accomplishes it apart from our awareness.

It is against the background of his work with symbol and metaphor that Ricoeur develops his hermeneutics of narrative. The interrelations among language, temporality, and world all come, again, into play. As with symbol and metaphor, narratives are not for Ricoeur occasional products of language but bring to attention aspects of language that are more generally true but not always noticeable.

A principal characteristic of narrative is that its events are not discrete but related. Attention to narrative, "story-following," is the process of trying to understand what has already happened by finding out what will happen next. Events not only lead to or cause one another; they also reveal the meaning of previous events by revealing their consequences. This aspect of story-following is true not only of attention to narrative; discourse is always unified in this way. It is so because this is how human temporality itself is unified.[48]

The process of story-following can be more exactly described, according to Ricoeur, by noting that narrative plot has two aspects. On the one hand, plot has an episodic aspect: That is, plot includes a series of isolatable incidents and episodes. One can, in reflecting on a story, remember certain moments. But along with this episodic aspect and never divorced from it there is in plot a configurational aspect. This aspect gives rise to the unity, wholeness, or significance of the events. It is not as though we move, in story-following, from one event to the next; rather, we are carried along by an unfolding design that grants to all the events their particular relevance to the whole. Narratives reveal a unity, then, between the momentary and the extended in human temporality, between incidents and an inclusive direction or meaning.[49]

Ricoeur formulates this theory of narrative in opposition to two theories that themselves stand as contraries to one another. One is provided by the structural orientations of Propp, Lévi-Strauss, Roland Barthes, and A. J. Greimas. It stresses the constant, the whole, even the static in narrativity as it stresses *langue* over *parole* in language theory. On the other side are empiricist understandings of human events as inherently discrete. The application of the model of physical to human events denies, as structuralists from the other, more idealistic side deny, the indissoluble unity in narrativity and human temporality between individual events and the larger patterns of which they are a part, to which they contribute and from which they derive their meaning.[50]

The stress on the unity in narrative between the episodic and the configurational undergirds as well Ricoeur's understanding of the unity and interdependence between historical and fictional narratives. Indeed, at times it is difficult to make a clear break between the two, since they overlap. However, they can be differentiated by their contrary emphases. Ricoeur, following Aristotle, describes historical narratives as adhering to events, subjecting narrative to the depiction of what actually occurred. Fictional narratives, on the other hand, are more philosophical—freer, that is, to depict possible events or what is always happening. Another way in which Ricoeur distinguishes between historical and fictional narrative is to say that fictional narrative, like metaphor, subverts or violates our sense of what actually happened, even of what does happen, in order to reveal something hidden or new in human life. This means that fictional and historical narratives require, and have their special roles clarified in distinction from, one another.

II

When the hermeneutical theories of Gadamer and Ricoeur are employed toward a method of narrative analysis, care must be taken not to falsify their position toward literature. It is not as though a narrative stands before the critic as a discrete object with only internal relations to analyze. For both Gadamer and Ricoeur a work of literary art stands out not because it is unrelated to language, experience, and world but because it is so meaningfully related to them. It epitomizes or brings to attention what is generally the case. The move from their theories to the next question—

What in narrative does critical hermeneutics bring most clearly into view?—should not leave this characteristic of their work behind.

The answer to the question is different from what might be expected. Because of the influence on them of Martin Heidegger's work and its attempt to reveal temporality as fundamental to human existence and to our understanding of it, we could expect that theories of Gadamer and Ricoeur would be most immediately applicable to narrative plot. Indeed, Ricoeur in his narrative theory is largely, one could almost say exclusively, attentive to plot. In his recent book on fictional narrative, the second volume of his three-part study *Time and Narrative,* Ricoeur takes up character and point of view, but he treats these not as elements of narrative of equal importance to plot but as aspects of narrative that complicate and expand the nature of plot and that must be understood in relation to plot or action. And while he often refers in the study to "world," to the world of the work or of the text and to the imagined or narrated "world," he does not take this "world" or what is responsible within a narrative for it as an element of the form.[51] His work, however, as does also that of Gadamer, leads, I believe, past plot to narrative atmosphere, howevermuch he does not or would not recognize that direction in his theory of narrative.

The move toward atmosphere can already be anticipated in the understanding of human temporality. Again the influence of Heidegger becomes clear. The principal dimension of time for both Gadamer and Ricoeur is the future. True, the future is related to the past and the present and has no meaning without them. But nothing is so definitive for human life as its future-orientation. Life itself, like story-following, is primarily an orientation to what will happen next.

The future is so intriguing because it holds, according to Gadamer and Ricoeur, the promise of expanding meaning. Meaning arises from the situation of conflict or offense in the anticipation of new meaning. Meaning is created by first being threatened. New meaning occurs beyond the threat when a common ground between differing parties emerges. The impasse, the threat, directs attention to the future. Furthermore, this future is not so much temporal as it is spatial. That is, what can be hoped for in the moment of conflict, impasse, or threat is a realm large enough to contain the value of both or all parties in the situation of conflict. This spatial quality of the future is suggested in the images used by Gadamer and Ricoeur in referring to it: "world" and "horizon."

Perhaps an example will make this matter clearer. The situation of impasse or conflict occurs, for example, when one realizes that another party in a conversation, for reasons of age, sex, or ethnic and religious identity, does not understand what has been said or else differs strongly as to how something should be understood or judged. One response to this situation, of course, is to end the conversation. Another is to overpower the other point of view with arguments defending the sole validity of one's own. A third response would be to compromise, to affirm that both may partially contribute to a resolution acceptable to both but wholly incorporating the contribution of neither. Gadamer and Ricoeur hold out for yet another possibility: the affirmation of both points of view as components of a larger, as yet unrealized, encompassing whole.

In other words, impasse, conflict, and threat are the means by which human worlds open up to a more inclusive horizon by which parties that differ can be included. More than that, there is implied in their work an affirmation of the comprehensiveness, the capaciousness, of this horizon. To encounter difference as a good thing, to take the violation of expectation as a prelude to greater meaning, is to have faith in a larger world before such a world appears.

The stress in the work of Gadamer and Ricoeur on temporality, therefore, depends upon something more basic, namely, a faith that the boundaries or conditions of life are of a certain receptive, elastic, or inclusive nature. The future is affirmed because of its inexhaustible commodiousness. This future is, furthermore, more discontinuous from a person's or group's past or present than Ricoeur and Gadamer take into account. For the future upon which time depends is not somebody's or some group's future; it is a kind of fourth dimension of time, as Heidegger would put it, a kind of nontemporal reality that houses time.[52] This other kind of future remains hidden until impasse or conflict offends the particular future of a person or group and persons or groups allow their own future to yield to the new possibility.

The primacy of the conditions of life, of the transcendent or hidden world by which the human enterprise is housed, of this encompassing horizon, relates the work of Gadamer and Ricoeur more to narrative atmosphere than to plot. Atmosphere, that aspect of setting that defines the conditions of the narrative world and determines what in it is or is not possible, directly relates to the principal orientation of Gadamer and Ricoeur to "world." Atmosphere is that element principally responsible for granting a narrative a "world," of establishing, that is, the horizon of conditions or possibilities under or within which life in the narrative is carried on.

III

Returning to the discussion of the Book of Jonah with these comments concerning Gadamer and Ricoeur in mind, we attend to the atmosphere of the narrative with more interest than before. Of special importance is the fact that the boundaries of the narrative world differ from what Jonah assumes the boundaries of the world to be. The atmosphere of the narrative world is more capacious than the "atmosphere" of the world in which Jonah considers himself to be living.

At first there is a violation of the boundaries of Jonah's world. Yahweh's favor is to be extended to the Ninevites. Yahweh is not limited to a world out of which Jonah can sail. The negative experiences in the narrative, the storm, imprisonment in the great fish, and the oppressive heat, expose Jonah to forces he cannot control or from which he cannot protect himself. But these violations and negative qualities of the borders of Jonah's world allow him to experience, even though he does not always understand or appreciate it, the larger world that includes but is not limited to his.

This larger world is also one that unifies Israel's distant past and its remote future. The world of the narrative is both forward and backward looking. It also affirms the validity of all three of the differing interests in the Old Testament: priestly, prophetic, and sapiential. And, more important, it establishes that both Israel and Nineveh, however distant and different from one another they may be, live in a world neither of them comprehends either politically or religiously. Yet, and this may be the most important factor to consider, the narrative brings together these separated or differing components without making clear the basis upon which their differences are part of a larger whole.

The atmosphere of Jonah also unifies two contrary functions of language and narrative: to establish and to subvert a world. Karl Mannheim calls these two functions ideological and utopian.[53] The ideological is that function by which language and narrative grant people a particular, stable world in which to carry on the normal course of life. The human enterprise depends upon such stability. Further, language and narrative grant this stability a certain legitimacy. But language and narrative have another, contrary function, and this is to subvert, to challenge, this granted world in the name of another, larger and more meaningful possibility.

Generally these two functions of language and narrative, these two interests or orientations—ideological and utopian—are taken to be exclusive of one another. But the narrative of Jonah reveals that they are parts of a larger whole. For the narrative is at one time both ideological and utopian. On the one hand, it is strongly affirmative concerning the people, their history, and relation to Yahweh. It represents a summary of Israel's history, a respect for its texts, and an emphasis on its particular soteriological role in the world. On the other hand, the narrative subverts this world and its specialness for a potentially larger and more meaningful one. Yahweh does not forsake Jonah, despite the prophet's failure to understand and appreciate the larger picture. Nor can the reader be sure how the particular and the general, one people and other peoples, establishment and disestablishment, are related to one another. What the atmosphere of Jonah means, finally, is that living in a world whose conditions are divinely established results both in having a world and having that world taken away. The narrative grants an unarticulated unity to the dynamic interactions of these contraries.

Finally, atmosphere in Jonah identifies the basis for trusting the horizon of life as an infinitely expandable and inclusive one. That basis is Yahweh himself, for, as Jonah makes clear in his confessional description, Yahweh knows no boundaries (4:2). A tension develops in the narrative, then, between these two very different poles, between Jonah, who, like all people, needs boundaries in order to have identity, and Yahweh, who has and needs no boundaries. The moment of an expanded horizon, therefore, a sense of moving into a larger world, is a revelatory or mediating moment between these contrary positions in relation to boundaries, the human and the divine.

Composition Criticism

The fourth approach to biblical narrative has, in comparison to the others, less self-consciousness regarding both scholarly or theoretical backing and method. This may be due to an assumption that interest in the concerns and the craft of the author is what literary criticism, after all, really is. Because of this assumption, furthermore, composition criticism may also appear less partial than it is. But as Meir Sternberg's recent major study, *The Poetics of Biblical Narrative,* makes clear, this approach is indebted to or is fueled by communication theory. It is, as he says, a "discourse-oriented analysis" of narrative.[54] This means that composition criticism is oriented primarily to tone, and it takes the narrative as a whole to be "a network of clues to the speaker's intention."[55]

This method, when applied to biblical narrative, encounters difficulties, however. Not only is so little known about the authorship of biblical narratives, but the authors also seem to delight not only in concealing their identities but also in creating narrators, as Sternberg puts it, different from and, by virtue of privilege or access to knowledge, closed to their historical creators, whoever they may have been.[56]

Since, in biblical narratives, the narrator is distant not only from his or her material but from the reader, and even from the author, the tasks of biblical criticism of this kind are necessarily more formal and intrinsic than they would be for other kinds of texts. It becomes necessary to infer from the texts the general linguistic and narrative situation in which the author works. It then becomes possible to describe both the constraints which that situation imposes on the author and to distinguish from them decisions that appear to indicate the author's own moves within those constraints.

Another characteristic of composition criticism is that it is less controversial in the forum of biblical studies than those discussed so far because it appears to be similar to a kind of scholarship that has become a standard part of biblical studies, namely, redaction criticism. Biblical scholarship itself has been concerned, especially since the 1950s, with the authors or editors of texts and has sought to characterize what their particular interests have contributed to the selection, coloring, and shaping of material. Redaction critics assume that the existing text comprises an original assortment of smaller units altered and combined to fit a larger, intentional purpose. The orientation of redaction criticism to the process of editing and shaping allows composition criticism to appear as a less provocative literary method to biblical scholars than the other three kinds. The similarities to redaction criticism, however, begin to fade when the orientation of composition criticism becomes clearer. Composition criticism is more concerned than is redaction criticism with something inherent within the narrative, something without which the narrative could not exist. Redaction criticism assumes that there is a narrative or an assortment of short narratives already present when the work of the redactor begins. Composition criticism would assume not only that the making of narratives out of shorter narratives is nothing unusual, that such always goes on, but also that the shorter narratives themselves have tellers within them. The teller for composition criticism is more enfolded within the completed narrative than external to it; redaction criticism is not so careful to avoid the impression of the author or editor as standing outside of the narrative or of the units that constitute it.

To say that composition criticism is oriented to tone means that it is attentive to three aspects of the narrative. The first is material selection. The reader receives, however consciously, a sense of the teller's presence by having to rely on, and being limited to, what the teller has chosen or feels required to narrate. Second, the teller has a certain attitude toward this material. This attitude has two aspects; the physical attitude means that the teller stands in a certain relation to the material, outside or inside it as one of the characters, near or distant. This aspect of the teller's presence is generally referred to as point of view. The other aspect of attitude is emotional or evaluational. The teller has a certain regard for the material—praise or disdain, for example. Third, the teller is recognizable by voice, by language choice.

I

One of the ways in which composition criticism becomes less personal, less an emphasis on the intentions and abilities of the author, and more oriented to ways in which the teller is determined, is by turning to the language or culture as a kind of teller. Material, attitude toward it, and voice are also marks of a culture or language. The constraints of a particular culture or language determine what will be narrated and what not, what stressed and what neglected, what viewed as close and what as far. True, this kind of criticism is bound to be tentative, since it is very difficult to characterize a culture as a kind of teller with certain predilections and values, possibilities and limitations. But attempts have been made and should be mentioned. Primarily these attempts have been marked by a comparison between the language and culture of biblical narrative and those of some other narrative corpus. For example, there have been several attempts to trace the characteristics of the collective or communal teller in biblical narratives by comparing them with Greek literature.

A well-known example of this kind is Eric Auerbach's essay "Odysseus' Scar." His principal point of contrast between Hebrew and Greek narratives concerns their contrary evaluation of background and foreground. For example, Homer presents a specificity of location that is absent in the stories about Abraham. The *Odyssey* stresses physical details; as much as possible is brought into the foreground. The style represents phenomena "in a fully externalized form, visible and palpable in all their parts and completely fixed in their spatial and temporal relations."[57] Even psychological processes are vented in speech. What is most characteristic, in contrast to Hebrew narrative, Auerbach contends, is the lack of gaps, the absence of unnarrated background. Consequently, Homeric epics are most suited to the depiction of physical action.

The Abraham stories present, Auerbach thinks, a quite different situation. When God speaks to Abraham we have little if any indication of Abraham's location and circumstances. Details, when provided, have more of an ethical than a physical import. For example, we are told that when Abraham sets off to sacrifice Isaac he arises early in the morning. But this detail is included not so much for the sake of temporal setting, a physical situation, as to convey Abraham's moral readiness to carry out the divine command. The text recounts, furthermore, little of the trip that Abraham and his son make that day, and we are given few of their thoughts. So much is *not* narrated. Auerbach concludes, therefore, that the material selection characteristic of Hebrew narrative differs from that of Greek in that in biblical stories the tellers give us very little of the surface detail of situations, events, and characters.

This difference is also indicated, according to Auerbach, by the fact that Homer's heroes have little behind them in the sense of history. They seem to awaken each morning as though to the first day of their lives. The pasts of their Hebrew counterparts, in contrast, weigh heavily on them. A biblical character stands in an ongoing narrative of tensions, precedents, and destinies. This sense of an ongoing story in which the biblical characters take a part grants, along with absence of physical detail, a sense of background to Hebrew narrative that is not the principal orientation of Greek narrative.

Auerbach also contends that Homeric characters are placed primarily in relation to other characters, while biblical figures are placed more frequently in vertical relations with the presence or the promises and laws of God. This pressure on them of divine investment also grants a significance to background that stands in contrast to Greek narrative.

Finally, Auerbach finds a point of contrast between the two kinds of narrative orientation in the degree of stability and instability evidenced by Greek and Hebrew characters and situations. Homeric characters are more stable than their Hebrew counterparts. Abraham, for example, fluctuates widely in a rather brief narrative span; he moves from moments of intimacy with God to times of disregard for his own special calling and place. He is both a person of great stature and heroism and a person vulnerable to self-compromise and folly. Auerbach contends that this difference appears not only in character depiction; the social, economic, and political situations in which biblical characters live are less stable than those of settings in Greek narrative. Abraham hardly knows from one day to the next, it seems, how his flocks will fare, and he is tossed about in political situations over which he has little control. In the world of Homer, in contrast, the characters live in a world that is made constant by the investments of deities in it. The Greek world is substantially more ordered and fully articulated than that of Hebrew narratives, which are more given to disruptions and less fully realized.

Criticism of this kind is provocative for two reasons. It attempts to draw sharp distinctions between large bodies of material, and the attempt is bound to stimulate the citation of exceptions. In addition to the generality of this critical method, there is also an implication in it of determinism rather than choice. This also arouses protest, and a good example of it is the response of James Barr, in his *Semantics of Biblical Language,* to attempts by Thorlief Boman to compare Greek with Hebrew narratives.[58] Barr attacks Boman's book for being too limiting and too generalizing in its contrasts. While Boman's work may be vulnerable to such criticism, we should recognize in it another attempt to characterize the teller in Hebrew narrative as determined by the constraints and orientations of a specific culture and language. It is an interesting form of composition criticism.

For Boman the mind that one encounters in Greek literature is determined by a language emphasizing stasis, space, and sight rather than, as with Hebrew, movement, time, and hearing. Boman carries this distinction throughout his study by contrasting Greek and Hebrew verbs, concepts of the nature of language and of speech, attitudes toward completed action in contrast to action in process, and differing understandings of the nature of transcendence.[59] The kind of contrast Boman makes between these two kinds of collective tellers, what he calls "minds," is made by others as well. Hans Jonas, for example, analyzes the epistemology of ancient Greece in terms of the pervasive metaphors of seeing and of light in relation to knowing. Sight stresses simultaneity and physical relations between entities at rest. Hearing, which is more important for biblical narratives, creates wholes out of temporal sequences. Sight minimizes temporality, while a stress on hearing requires it.[60]

The question raised by Barr's attack on Boman's work is not whether work of this kind convincingly contrasts two "minds" but whether or not such differences in collective tellers exist. Can one say that Hebrew narrative differs from Greek in material selection, in attitude toward the material, and in the way the story is told? The answer of composition criticism to such a question must always be yes, for if there are such differences between narratives within a culture there must, *a fortiori*, be such differences between narratives of differing cultures. The search for ways of describing these differences arouses suspicion and may create offense because of a contrary, also legitimate interest. Barr represents one example of it, the interest, often to be found among historians, to protect a period or a culture from the limitations, even the caricatures, of those who describe it as a whole, apparently neglecting its diversity and details. Cultures and epochs distant from one's own often appear less complex than they actually are or were. Distance simplifies. However, another legitimate interest is to describe in some way how a culture, despite its complexity, is particularized, even limited. This is important for the understanding of narrative, for narratives have a particularity of teller, however collective that teller may be. All narratives are somebody's. Particularity is cultural as well as individual. The distinctions between Greek and Hebrew narratives that Auerbach, Boman, and Jonas are attempting to make are based on the assumption that cultural particularity is determinative. This particularity affects the narratives of a culture from root to branch. Resistance to their attempts may reflect a desire to protect a culture from the limits that particularity implies.

While it may not be possible to say how and where biblical narratives are culturally particular, attempts to do so should not be intimidated by the kinds of interests, legitimate in themselves, that Barr represents.

II

Attention to the teller in the tale, to narrative tone, leads most directly, of course, to questions concerning the individual author's presence in a narrative. While this question would seem easier to handle because it is more specific than the question of the image of a particular culture present in the telling of a narrative, it is not less elusive. In fact, the two questions are related. If it were possible to understand the particularity of the cultural "teller" embedded in biblical narratives, the image of the individual teller could be more easily distinguished in its particularity from or within it.

The situation is also made difficult by the fact that biblical narratives are often communal and traditional. Many have been passed down over generations and thereby lose the individuality that a story with a single teller would have. We also cannot often be certain what the conventions within a tradition of storytelling were, so that individuality, the deviations from and improvisations on such conventions, could be detected whenever it occurs. It is difficult to isolate individuality and artistry when one cannot measure them by some sense of what is conventional and derivative. Complicating this situation even more is the fact that modern readers may place far more value on the role of tone in narrative than the ancients did, more value on the identification, even inclusion, of the narrator within the narrative. Biblical narrative seems to delight in the concealment of the narrator; indeed, much of the artistry may lie precisely here, in the effect of not making the reader aware of a teller in the tale.

The concealment of the teller is accomplished in two ways, one of which has already been noted in this study whenever the subject of tone in biblical narratives arose. Point of view, an ingredient of tone, is generally omniscient in biblical narrative. So omniscient is it that the perspective of the teller often includes deity. The narrators are privy, for example, to conversations between Yahweh and individuals. The narrator also frequently knows what is stirring in the minds and hearts of characters and at times even how Yahweh feels about certain events and situations. The narrator would not be able to do all of this quite so easily if the reader were aware of the narrator as a particular person. For then the reader would want to know and would have to be told how information of this privileged kind came into the narrator's hands. When credentials of that sort are requested, the question of veracity and trustworthiness arises with it. But the question does not arise in biblical narrative, precisely because the narrator is not revealed as a particular person with a particular point of view and all of the limitations that attend to the question of perspective.

The matter of omniscient point of view in biblical narrative is a principal interest of Meir Sternberg's recent study. Replete with valuable observations concerning the tone of biblical narrative, Sternberg's book is particularly helpful in its convincing argument that the omniscient point of view, far from being accidental, is central to the ideology of the writers. The intention is to grant the narratives a certain authority by allowing the narrator to share a characteristic definitive of deity itself. "Within the Israelite reality-model, briefly, God stands opposed to humankind not so much in terms of mortality—after the fashion of both Orientals and Greeks—as in terms of knowledge." Biblical narratives, by means of omniscient point of view, have built within them "the cognitive antithesis between God and humanity."[61] Even when information concerning plot and character is withheld, it is not with the effect of indicating the limitation of the teller but of enhancing the mystery of tone.[62]

The concealment of the teller is accomplished not only by omniscience but also by what could be called a "historical effect." That is, the narrator works in such a way that the reader's attention is directed not to the teller and the teller's imagination, skill, or personal interests but to the material. Not only that; the reader thinks that what is related actually occurred, even when events described are marvelous. Readers of biblical narrative take this realistic effect so for granted that they may forget what artistry it requires. It is no different from the craftsmanship of a painter who can make the viewer think that the particulars of a still life are real. The effects in painting are dependent upon shading, contrasts, and color choices. Similarly, the reader of biblical narrative is "tricked" into thinking that what is narrated actually occurred. This in no way implies a judgment as to whether or not what is narrated did occur. Rather, it means only that the effect of biblical narrative is to draw attention not to the narrator but to the narrated and to lead the reader to

believe that what is told occurred. This takes skill. A less able narrator, even if dealing with events that actually occurred, may easily
fail in the attempt to convey the sense of actuality.

This realistic quality of biblical narrative is all the more surprising because the events that occur often stand in an ontological
situation above the reader's. The world that the reader inhabits is a
world often different from that which the narrative presents. Wonderful things occur in the narrative that do not occur in the world
of the reader: Elderly people, past the years of childbearing, have
babies; waters are parted so that the people can safely pass on dry
land; the walls of a city fall; prophets raise children from death;
and individuals have conversations with deities and heavenly mes-
sengers. In biblical narrative the teller gives us material that stands
at an ontological and evaluational level above the reader. Furthermore, by knowing so much about that world, the narrator presents
him or herself as a part of it, so that the teller is as much above the
world of the reader as an inhabitant of it. The teller is a kind of
mediator between the world of the narrative and the world of the
reader.

It may also be possible to point to marks of tone in biblical narrative that are more specific than these concerning omniscient point
of view, the realistic effects, and the narrator's participation in or
access to an ontologically superior world. A recent attempt to be
more specific is Robert Alter's *Art of Biblical Narrative*. Alter thinks
it is possible to detect intentions within the narratives that create
particular effects. He approaches biblical narratives with the assumption that the consequences of authorial choices and their art-
ful effects can be found in them.

Alter addresses the problem of distinguishing individual artistry
from the background of convention by noting both recurring type-
scenes and verbal repetitions. For example, such scenes as the an-
nouncement of a birth, the search for a wife, an epiphany in a field,
or the testament of a dying father can be detected as conventional.
The artistry of biblical narrative, the presence of the teller, appears
in the liberties taken with these conventional components of the
story. While Alter is not sanguine about the ability of modern readers to understand the conventions so well that individual depar-
tures from them can be readily recognized, he argues that the
interaction of dependence on and departure from convention can
be detected. Alter also discovers individual artistry in the uses of

the *Leitwort* and motif, the explorations by the artists of the semantic range of particular words within a story and of recurring images, such as stones in the Jacob story, water in the narratives concerning Moses, and fire in the Samson tales.[63]

Alter observes, furthermore, that much of the artistry of biblical narratives lies within dialogue, because dialogue, more than description, bears the burden of revealing character. The conversations between Saul and David, for example, reveal the author's sense of the psychological makeup of the two figures and their resulting contrast. This dialogue is generally direct, and descriptive material of a scene, for example, or encounter, rather than a matter of interest in itself, serves to provide an occasion for dialogue.[64]

It may be possible to continue from Alter's point on the interrelation between characters to observe that another feature of characterization in the art of biblical narrative is the use of two figures who sharply contrast in the courses of their lives. We have this, of course, in the contrasting lines of development between Saul and David. A similar pattern can be seen in the contrast between Abraham and Lot. The separation between them establishes these two as representing contrasting styles of life, Lot's leading to increasing weakness and compromise. Cain and Abel, Esau and Jacob, Moses and Aaron, Elijah and Elisha—there are enough pairs and contrasts to suggest a reliance of biblical narrative on this device to reveal contrast and continuity between characters.

Returning to Alter, one more point, perhaps his most controversial, should be mentioned. He takes the juxtaposition of two stories concerning a single set of events to be intentional. For example, the inclusion in Genesis of two accounts of creation is not the consequence simply of splicing varying traditions but is also the consequence of a decision to create a certain effect, a kind of third dimensionality.[65] So, too, the differing accounts of David's introduction to Saul, the one by means of his musical abilities and the other by means of his fight with Goliath, have the effect of suggesting not only the contrast in David's character between the artist and the physical hero but also the complex nature of Saul's attraction to David. The reader, by not having the differences in two accounts of the same set of events resolved, is granted a sense of complexity and depth that a smoother narrative would lack. Indeed, the artistry of biblical narrative appears to be closely tied to the productive uses of roughness, incompleteness, and even contradiction in narrative. Rather than find this a problem, a sign of incompetence, or a slavish deference to varying sources, the modern reader should view it as an invitation to read the narratives appropriately.

III

The consequences of composition or artistry criticism for a reading of the Gospel According to Mark are available in a recent book by Frank Kermode, *The Genesis of Secrecy*. Kermode, like Alter, understands what readers may otherwise think of as textual problems or the results of sundry sources to be deliberate strategies of the teller designed, Kermode believes, to produce, among other effects, primarily the retention of meaning. Kermode takes the problem passages and puzzles in the Gospel, rather than its clearer, more coherent aspects, as central to an understanding of its author's intentions.

Kermode uses as an example the apparently gratuitous inclusion in the passion segment of the Gospel of the young man who flees naked from the soldiers. This curious, unexplained item is unintegrated into the segment. The reader is not told the identity of the young man nor why his presence and hasty departure are significant. Such a detail, a break in the sequential coherence of the narrative, has the effect not of threatening the meaning of the narrative, Kermode argues, but of adding to it. The reader is led to think that the event has a special meaning precisely because it is puzzling. A loose end such as this cannot be explained away by appeal to an actual occurrence, to the rough and detailed nature of life itself, or to the sources and materials with which the narrator is working. Narratives create, press for, wholes, and it goes against the grain of narrative to allow such a detail to stand out unintegrated. The cause, according to Kermode, is the author's intention to create in the narrative a sense of greater meaning than what is immediately available.[66]

According to Kermode, the intention of the narrator is to write a narrative that will be laden with inexhaustible, elusive meaning. The messianic secret, for example, a problem in interpreting the Gospel, does not point to a confusion either in the mind of the narrator or in the attitude of Jesus. Such puzzles are woven into the narrative so that the effects of uncertainty, of the unresolved, can be indefinitely maintained. Readers, rather than ignore such conundrums, are attracted to them and impute to them a meaning for the whole that eludes their grasp. This effect is intentional. The author of the Gospel wants, Kermode argues, to write meaning-packed but meaning-retentive narrative. He wants, in fact, to write scripture.[67]

Contraries and metaphorical rather than sequential relations also help to realize this intention. The Gospel is marked by many contraries: manifest/hidden, public/private, dying/living, now/the time to come, clean/unclean, recognition/denial. These contraries stimulate the reader to seek a formula by which they are to be reconciled. They serve both to engage the reader and to put the reader off, both to suggest a hidden meaning concerning their resolution and to refuse to give up that meaning. Such an intention generates mystery, and mystery fascinates the reader. The Gospel According to Mark is taken by Kermode as a primer in the strategies of meaning retention.[68]

Kermode's treatment of tone in the Gospel According to Mark gives us a narrative that is both simple and complicated, clear and puzzling, complete and abruptly incomplete (Mark 16:8). Another cause of these effects, I think, is that the narrative presents as unified matters that the reader would otherwise think of as unrelated: divine intention and human experience, the mundane and the transcendent, the temporal and the eternal, the Jesus of history and the Resurrected Lord. It may not be so much that the narrator wants to be puzzling as that the narrator uses these strategies to keep in view the mystery of the material with which he or she is dealing. This material does not articulate the unity between contrary realms of reality but discloses an underlying unity despite the apparent separation between them.

Only speculation can offer reasons and occasions for the Gospel having been written as it is. One may be able to say that the narrator was writing for a people who are accustomed to pilgrimage to Jerusalem but who no longer are able, because of the political situation, to engage in this rite. The narrative itself may be offered as a kind of pilgrimage. Or the author may be writing for people distressed by some form of persecution, people who consequently may have concluded that the heavenly and the earthly, human experience and divine intention, are unrelated. The intention within the narrative may be to comfort and to reassure the reader that despite appearances these realms are continuous with one another. The genesis of secrecy, to use Kermode's title, may lie in the material and the narrator's evaluation of it rather than, as Kermode implies, in the narrator's desire to gain a certain stature for the narrative. And this material selection or evaluation of it, along with an omniscient, future-positioned perspective, is the chief mark of the narrator's presence in the story.

Summary

The methodological variety of the literary interests in biblical narrative should not be bewildering. The four selected kinds—myth criticism, structural analysis, critical hermeneutics, and composition criticism—arise not only from varying scholarly interests but also from the complexity of the narrative form, and each addresses primarily one of the form's elements. The complexity of methods is due to the difficulty of being attentive equally and at the same time to all of the elements of narrative—so inclusive and interesting is each of the elements by itself. While it would not do to say that each of the four methods is *limited* to one of the elements, it is possible to say that each method is particularly well suited to treat one rather than some other of the elements of narrative: myth criticism, plot; structural analysis, character; critical hermeneutics, atmosphere; and composition criticism, tone.

Using the narrative form as a starting point, then, it is possible to affirm a critical pluralism that is not the consequence of methodological indecisiveness but is based on the nature of narrative and the capacity of each of its elements to dominate. The alternative to pluralism is the distortion to the narrative form that would result from attributing permanent dominance to one of its elements.

The mistake of imputing permanent dominance to one of the elements of narrative is almost universally made. Critics and theorists reveal an overriding interest in character, plot, or tone. There is nothing objectionable about an exclusive interest in one or two of the elements of narrative. The error arises from the assumption, whether stated or implied, that the dominant interest in the criticism corresponds to the permanent hegemony in the form of one of the elements of narrative over the others. But narrative is not constant in that way. It is variable, and variation is caused by shifting dominants. It is hoped that these four critical methods serve to make the nature of narrative, on this score, clear.

4

Narrativity and Textuality

The four selected critical methods lead not only into the nature of narrative; they also lead, however unintentionally, into another equally complex and important matter, textuality. They serve to reveal that biblical narratives depend for their power and meaning both on their narrative form and on their textuality. Awkward as it may seem, it is possible, as we shall see, to say that biblical narratives are "highly textual."

More is meant by textuality, therefore, than the obvious fact that we encounter biblical narratives as texts. While textuality cannot be divorced from the status of this discourse as textual rather than oral, the textuality that affects narrativity is of a more complicated, less obvious kind. To understand it we should look once again at these methods of literary criticism and the textual characteristics of plot, character, atmosphere, and tone that they help to bring to light. We shall then be in a position to examine the characteristics of textuality more closely.

Textuality and Critical Theories

Much that interests myth critics in narrative actually concerns textuality. "Myth" refers to patterns of action that are always being retold, that stand behind or lie within the stories that we daily encounter. "Myth" means the constantly reappearing, particularly the patterns that grant coherence to the events and help to create plot. "Myth" is the constant within the variety of narrative plots.

At first it may appear that myth criticism, by stressing an always appearing pattern, is freeing narrative from textuality, because myth seems to be something more or other than any one narrative can contain even when that narrative is a myth, a narrative, let us say, of the origins of the cosmos. Myth critics seem always to dissociate myth from the texts of particular stories. This is especially true of those who postulate some all-inclusive myth, only parts of which are present in any particular narrative—the seasonal, cyclical pattern of plots that Northrop Frye describes, for example, or the pattern of the hero's total journey that we have in Joseph Campbell's narrative theory. Indeed, such critics appear to free plot from the narrative texts and to ground it in something cosmic, psychological, or social. But while they seem to free myth from text, myth critics actually define myths in terms of textual characteristics.

By finding similar patterns in sundry narratives, myth critics draw attention to what in a narrative is transportable or importable. They reveal the interdependence of narratives. The consequences, the issues of this interdependence, are taken by myth critics as independent and originating. But it is first of all to the dependence of narratives on the repeatability of plot patterns, rather than to the nature or origins of those patterns themselves, that myth criticism as a literary method points.

Myth critics, when they define myth as the recurring in literature, as that which is always reappearing, draw attention not so much to myth, to a particular kind of narrative, as to textuality. Analogous to the way in which the many events of a narrative, despite gaps between them, are granted coherence by a recognizable, "followable" pattern, the many narratives we encounter are vulnerable to what Mircea Eliade calls an "eternal return." A reciprocity occurs between the coherence of a particular narrative and what could be called, perhaps, the narrative tradition. This reciprocity, this permeability between narratives, allows myth critics to abstract from narratives that which is both mobile between them and that which seems to grant a housing to many, if not all, narratives. They then project this pattern not as a composite but as an original whole, and grant it some kind of cosmic, sociological, or psychological reality.

The dependence of myth criticism on textuality does not discount this form of literary interest. Rather, it leads us to recognize that textuality always impinges upon our relation to and understanding of a narrative. Narrativity depends for its force and meaning as much on permeability and interdependence as upon particularity and nonconformity. And all narratives have a potential place in the larger narrative "world" that shared coherence provides. For this reason, knowledge of many stories can make us aware that despite the multiplicity and diversity among them we may constantly be hearing similar stories, one story from among a limited set, or parts of a large, single story. The familiar, the recognizable in a narrative, is, in fact, fundamental to the apprehension of a story heard for the first time. Much of the delight in the reception of narratives arises from a tacit comparison that is carried on between the familiar and what is new or from a recognition of how in this narrative the familiar is being altered or subverted. While too much permeability in a narrative will make it too familiar, not particular enough, too little will make it difficult to follow. The power and meaning of a narrative must be found somewhere between the repeated and the new, the familiar and the strange.

Structural analysis also draws attention to the role of textuality in narrative. The move from a particular narrative to a system or repertoire behind it imputes to the system a status and a function similar to those imputed by myth critics to myth. The difference between myth criticism and structural analysis on this point is not that the one turns to story and the other to system but that myth critics turn to plot, to the pattern that grants coherence to events, while structural analysts are more oriented to discrete units and their relations in the narrative. Characters, or what Greimas refers to as *actants,* are the most likely candidates.

Like myth critics, structural analysts appear to minimize textuality, for they prefer a system behind the narrative to the narrative text itself. What is more, they impute to this abstraction a nontextual nature, for it exists beneath discourse, even beneath awareness. Structural analysts appear to discount textuality for something pretextual. However, the characteristics that they impute to the system are derived from that which narratives share. The system is actually an abstraction from narratives, from the consequences of intertextuality, and a projection of these consequences on some postulated ground or level behind or beneath them.

This move on the part of structural analysts of taking recurring units in narratives and projecting them as a nontextual, prediscursive system does not discount the importance of their work. For they, too, draw attention to the fact that much of our relation to narrative depends upon its depiction of individual characters or roles as variations on a particular kind of character or role and how they are established and clarified by patterns of antagonism and support or similarity and difference. This projection of the textual within character allows us to recognize the dependence of narrative on textuality, on the play of variation and particularity in characterization against a background of what is recurring and constant within character depiction. Characters in a narrative have power and meaning because of an interplay between the constant and the varying, the stable and the idiosyncratic. And narrative as a form of discourse depends for its intelligibility on the relations that can be drawn between many characters and a more limited set of types, qualities, or roles.

The intertextuality of narrativity to which myth criticism and structural analysis direct us presents the characteristics of textuality as though they stand behind or below the narrative; myth and system appear, as it were, as patterns and structures of coherence that one detects by looking through the narrative. Another way of saying this is that plot and character are those elements that relate narrative to textuality primarily as though to something behind it or in the past. The remaining two kinds of criticism call attention to the relations of narrative to textuality as to something ahead of narrative or to something in the narrative's future. They do so because they emphasize the role of textuality in narrative atmosphere and tone.

The principal orientation of critical hermeneutics to atmosphere, to the "ontological world" or horizon of possibilities by which contraries are housed, places great weight on the future. A question must be raised concerning this horizon. It seems to have a quite special meaning in the work of Gadamer and Ricoeur, to be a world, indeed, capacious enough to house, if not to transcend and interpret, differences within and between texts in terms that these texts themselves do not provide. In fact, it is precisely at the moment of failure, at the moment when it becomes clear that the terms for coherence between conflicting texts are not provided by them, that the future in its capacious but directed openness presents itself as horizon. This nontextual coherence stands to texts in a way analogous to the standing in Heidegger's work of Being to the existence of a person; it is in the sense of the limitation, even the ending, of life that the presence of Being can be felt.

However nontextual this horizon may be thought to be in the capaciousness that it offers texts in their limitations, the horizon itself is textual. What exists, otherwise, beyond the hermeneutical situation drawing the parties into an unarticulated, forward-directed coherence? This is a major matter, for in this critical method the task of interpretation is finally undertaken not for the sake of the texts but for the sake of that broader world that engagement with the otherness of texts will open up. That engagement creates and enlarges meaning. To answer the question we must work from the atmosphere of a particular narrative to the projection of atmosphere as a future housing for disparate texts.

Atmosphere is that element that grants the entities of a narrative a unified world. Dependent more upon spatial than upon temporal images, atmosphere grants to particulars in a narrative a common stage, a oneness or wholeness of world. The wholeness of world may, in some narratives, be severely taxed. When a narrative contains perspectives, situations, or characters not clearly related to one another or at the end unresolved, the sense of a single world may be strained. Despite the strain on wholeness, however, the reader will sense, if the world of the narrative is at all intelligible, that these various situations occur on a single stage or in one container. This sense of spatial wholeness atmosphere provides.

The atmosphere of a narrative, by which many, often contrary particulars are housed, is analogously related to that world or horizon of potential meaning to which critical hermeneutics draws attention and attests. That future is, I think, an extrapolation and a projection of the element of narrative that I have called "atmosphere." With all that the atmosphere of a particular narrative may carry with it as well, narrative atmosphere is related to a textual characteristic, an expectation of inclusiveness that is derived from textual experiences or transported from one text to another.

Critical hermeneutics relies on narrative atmosphere without recognizing that it has these textual qualities. Ricoeur seems more aware of the problem than Gadamer, for Ricoeur wants to avoid Hegelianism or idealism. For Ricoeur the existence of a broader world beyond texts, by which texts, despite the ways in which they conflict, are held within a single capacious horizon, is suggested by texts themselves through the polysemic nature of language. The overabundance of meaning in language, the refusal of language to be univocal or uni-directed, enables texts always to be more than they appear to be or than we take them to be. This means that a text's excess of meaning, which always eludes the grasp of readers, is opening up possibilities of a world in which it will stand in some kind of reconciliation with texts it now seems to contradict. The problem with Ricoeur's solution is that it involves him in a potential contradiction. The impasse that occurs when the interpretation of texts in conflict is not forthcoming is due, for Ricouer, to the range of semantic possibilities. There is a genuine impertinence, a genuine lack of meaning, in the hermeneutical situation that must be experienced before a new meaning, a broader horizon, appears. But Ricoeur cannot both deny the presence of the terms of resolution within the texts when he describes the moment of impertinence and then attribute the new pertinence to latent possibilities within the texts.

The question, then, can be put this way: Why is it not the case that impertinence will lead to confusion, that conflicts between texts will lead to a Babel of unrelated assertions? What prevents differences from producing an entropic state rather than an expanded world of meaning? The answer is that critical hermeneutics projects narrative atmosphere beyond the text of a particular narrative and construes the hermeneutical process as a grand, living narrative housed by an actual atmosphere or horizon of meaning. Critical hermeneutics projects the world-granting qualities of narrative atmosphere as a nontextual, receding reality.

This is not something that ought to be embarrassing. Gadamer and Ricouer fully recognize the past as a text that is always changing its meaning in relation to the ever-developing world of texts; so they should recognize the future as textual or the textual character of the future as well. This time the text is not, as Gadamer puts it, tradition; rather it is the text of expectation. Upon this text the hermeneutical process depends. Unity is created or adumbrated between texts or worlds that differ in the present by the text of expectation, of a future capacious enough to house them despite their differences. Critical hermeneutics, then, turns attention to textuality as ahead of or above texts, as in their future, while myth criticism and structural analysis turn attention to textuality as behind or beneath narratives, as in their pasts.

Tone and composition criticism are textually oriented toward the future, too. Tone, the presence of the teller in the narrative, that in the narrative that makes it someone's story, is produced by the choice of material, attitude toward it, and voice. The word "choice," of course, must be loosely taken, because the teller may feel compelled to relate certain material, may be forced by the material to take a certain attitude toward it, and may be required by vocabulary and degree of sophistication to speak with a particular "voice." Yet, we encounter a narrative as discourse in which choices have been made, and we are engaged by that to which those choices commit the teller or what commitments those choices reveal the teller to have.

These choices, obviously, belong to the past. At some point an author took the time to write a novel, let us say, and the results of decisions determine the novel's tone. But textuality, as recent reader-response criticism makes clear, allows the reader to experience these choices while reading, as though they are ahead. The reader, like Dante by Virgil, is led in the narrative by the teller. The teller knows the material and conducts the reader through it, influences responses by the physical and evaluative attitude held toward the material, and unifies material and attitude by a certain style. The reader is primarily oriented to the teller as to something in the future, something ahead. The teller, by holding a future position, always transcends, while being part of, the world of the narrative. Even if the narrator is a character in the narrative, the teller is always ahead of, always knows more than, the reader. The reader must wait for the teller to disclose what will happen next and receives only what the teller is willing and able to offer. In terms of the unfolding world of the narrative, then, the teller is always omniscient or ahead, even though that omniscience may be modified or concealed in a particular narrative.[1]

The concealment of omniscience is a common characteristic of twentieth-century fiction. Omniscience smacks of deity and authority, and ours is a relativistic age. But limited point of view is always a self-limitation, an artifice, because the teller, as regards the world of the narrative, does the limiting as to what shall be narrated and what not, chooses, in other words, the material.

Because the teller is always ahead of and knows more than the reader, the teller's attempts to conceal this position by placing the center of awareness not above the characters, for example, but within their consciousnesses are attempts actually to repress the textuality of narrative. It is as though a museum guide would pretend that he or she is conducting the tour for the first time, without plan, and has no more idea than those being guided what painting will be encountered next. The guide, by a certain fresh and lively manner, may conceal the fact that the whole of the tour is a text. What gives the appearance of nontextuality is actually a characteristic of textuality, namely, allowing the hearer or reader to start from the beginning and follow through to the end.

The orientation of composition critics to the author, to decisions made by the author and the consequences of those decisions, draws attention to the textuality upon which narrativity at the point of tone depends. This is true even though composition criticism appears to project these decisions into the past, into a kind of pretextual, originating moment. But those decisions that constitute a kind of text of expectation, a plan, move ahead of the narrative in dynamic counterpoint with its composition. Choices are constantly being made in the course of the narrative as to what should be included and what not (material), as to how this event or entity should be viewed (attitude), and what words should be used (voice). The author is as much ahead of the narrative, making choices, as behind it. And aheadness is a textual designation, that which lies in front of the text unfolded thus far. And it is this process that the reader follows and encounters as tone.

Narrative discourse and textuality, therefore, have much to do with one another. This is not because many of the narratives we encounter are written rather than spoken or because narratives that we consider authoritative or culturally formative, such as classical and biblical narratives, are written, but because all narratives rely on and play upon textuality. The coherence of a narrative's temporality will be recognizable because it will draw on, modify, or subvert a pattern of temporal coherence that myth critics refer to as "myth." In addition, the characters we encounter hold certain positions in the narrative, are in part recognizable because of their familiar qualities or roles. We appreciate their individuality when the characters stand out from their roles or qualities or fulfill and reveal them in unusual ways. A text of character types or functions stands behind our understanding and appreciation of narrative. No less does atmosphere rely on a text of expected relations between disparate interests and entities, relations that need not be wholly articulated. While narrative atmosphere provides a certain world, most obviously through setting, a spatial and temporal stage for the narrative, the sense of a unified world is dependent upon an expectation, a text concerning the future of or in front of the narrative. And the presence of a teller in the tale, the sense of being in the hands of a guide, is closely tied to textuality, to decisions being made and to the effect of decisions as the story is being told, an effect that the textuality of the narrative allows to be repeated endlessly.

Textuality and Biblical Narrative

The four critical methods, by granting access to the textuality of narratives, to their dependence on and contribution to what is stable, coherent, and repeatable in and between narratives, reveal, it seems to me, why their practitioners are drawn to biblical narratives. They are so drawn, along with whatever other reasons one could cite, because biblical narratives are highly textual. Rather than eschew textuality and its consequences, they exploit it, so that the power and meaning of biblical narratives arise from the characteristics of textuality as well as from those of narrativity. Indeed, biblical narratives reveal something about textuality, as they also reveal something about the narrative form.

Such characteristics of textuality as repeatability and stability are balanced in biblical narratives by an equal stress on particulars within a narrative and on the particularity of single narratives. The importance of textuality for biblical narratives does not minimize their equally strong emphasis on novelty and unpredictability. While biblical narratives exalt in textuality rather than repress it, they are also strongly individuated. Their plots often contain highly unusual, unexpected, or unprecedented events. Characters are frequently morally complex, idiosyncratic, and unpredictable. Atmosphere, while constricted by the particular situations depicted by the narratives, the "realistic" conditions in which life is carried on, is, at the same time, expanded by an array of characters and the often unresolved differences between them, and even by differing accounts of them. And the tone seems governed by a constant aim of presenting the material as uniquely significant. A particular person, people, and place, a unique role or significance assigned to this place or this event or this person—indeed, discontinuity, specialness, and particularity could not, it seems, be more fully emphasized than they are by these narratives. While attentive to the nature and consequences of textuality, no reader of biblical narrative should, perhaps even could, ignore the contrary exploitation of particularity. Indeed, the power and meaning of the narratives are not separable from this dual, even contrary, emphasis.

The Exodus narrative, as we saw, does not shun the role of textuality. The events of the narrative are generally preceded by a description Yahweh gives to Moses of what will occur. The script, so to speak, is read out before the action occurs. The formulas of the highly disruptive, chaotic events, of the plagues, structure them and grant a recurring coherence. And in the Passover textuality is fully emphasized. What the people do establishes a text, a set of actions that will provide a recurring, permanent pattern for people in the future to rehearse.

Not only this—it is possible to say that, within the particular story of a particular people brought from Egypt under the leadership of the man Moses, there is a more general, recurring pattern. It is the need people repeatedly reveal to be brought out of situations of deterioration and distress and to be given the freedom of a new beginning. More specifically, the terms of distress and deterioration are made constant, namely, the loss of meaning when events and their significance are dissociated and when the identity and integrity of a person or people are compromised by too close an association with and domination by others. People periodically need a reversal, an exchange of that situation for its contrary. This general pattern of loss and renewal stands with the particulars of the story, allowing it to be both a unique series of events and a pattern that has meaning for people vastly distant from such events and different from those for or to whom those events occur in the story.

This interplay between the constant and the varying or particular is also clear in the depiction of character in the Book of Judges. We are engaged by the individuality of the judges because there is behind them a text. The textual, that is, the unchanging function or office of deliverer laid down by the paradigm, stands in contrast to the individuality of those who perform or hold it. The result is a collection of particular characters who seem to have almost nothing at all in common. While we do not end with a clear idea of what a judge actually is or should be like, we have no doubt, because of the general pattern, that all of these people are appropriately related to one another by that office or role.

Here as elsewhere in biblical narrative there is a strong emphasis on the constancy that office or role provides. Spouse, parent, child, sibling, friend, warrior, leader, king, prophet, priest—people have their places. The interests of particularity do not slight the constancy of repeated, predictable offices and functions. And characters, by their individuality, give new meaning to the constant. We do not recognize Abraham only because he fulfills the function or plays the role of "father"; we recognize what fatherhood is because of Abraham.

In the Book of Jonah atmosphere is the consequence not only of those moments in which, by contradicting Jonah's wishes and actions, Yahweh brings him from a smaller to a larger world. It also provides the wholeness that contains the various interests or emphases of Israel's life, however much they may be in tension with one another: past and future, we and they, God as Creator of all and God as redeemer of a particular people, and the priestly, prophetic, and sapiential orientations.

However, the text does not resolve the principal tensions. For example, what does it mean for their futures that Israel and Nineveh both bow to the same God? The political and cultural consequences of the conversion of the Gentiles are not pursued. Yet the two peoples are now housed within a common world comprehended by the concern of Yahweh for them both. The spatial image of Yahweh's goodness as a horizon projected by the narrative ahead of itself, ahead of its ability to decribe the actual relation Nineveh and Israel are now to have, reveals the narrative's reliance on a text of expectation it cannot itself provide.

And the omniscient point of view in the Gospel According to Mark becomes a guide the reader is asked to follow. Not only does the narrator lead the reader through the material, granting judgments and carrying the reader's interests and understanding; the narrator also leads the reader beyond the narrative to where he or she is standing, beyond Jerusalem as the goal of pilgrimage, beyond a particular pilgrimage journey to the possibility of allowing one's own life to become a pilgrimage, a way of following, a kind of living and dying.

The role of textuality in biblical narratives raises a number of issues worth addressing. The first of these concerns dependence. Because the textuality of a narrative emphasizes the broader textual field of which it is a part and which it does not itself comprehend, this topic tends to reduce the self-enclosedness of biblical texts, their self-sufficiency. This means that biblical narratives are continuous with other narratives as well as different from them and unique. I do not merely mean that particular biblical narratives may be indebted to other ancient Near Eastern texts, as suggested by the relation the flood story holds to the Gilgamesh epic or to some other stories both may share. Rather, it means that the coherence and authority that the biblical narratives have and generate through their textuality cannot be thought of as appearing for the first time with them. Narrative always has a relation to a larger world of narrative, and biblical narratives do not, as we saw, try to deny that relationship. The textuality of narrative affirms extension as well as particularity. One can view this as dependence, a sign of weakness. I view it as strength, a sign of expansiveness. Something very important is lost from an appreciation of biblical narratives if their textuality, their participation in a broader narrative field, is neglected for the sake of their distinctiveness.

Furthermore, textuality reminds us of the transportability of biblical narratives. It not only means that people very different and distant from the time and setting of the narratives themselves can participate in their power and significance; it also means that biblical narratives can influence other narratives in ways and at levels that we cannot measure or even detect. That is, biblical narratives do not affect our own narratives only to the extent that they have explicit analogues in them to biblical situations, plots, or characters; our narrativity is always vulnerable to the effects of biblical narrative because of the more general field that their exploitation of textuality opens up to biblical narratives. Not only is it true that we cannot isolate biblical narratives from other narratives; we also cannot isolate other narratives from biblical texts. Because of what they do to and with textuality, biblical narratives continue to affect us. They have a double punch. They arrest us by their particularity, and, by their generality, they never let us go. Frank McConnell, introducing a recent collection of essays by literary and religious scholars, says that "the Bible *is* both the story of stories and the Text of texts."[2] That is, our interest in story and text, the very topics that draw contemporary critics and theorists to the Bible, is an interest that biblical narrative itself has created. No Western literature, in other words, no matter how antitraditional, antireligious, or antiformal, can escape the shaping of our culture, in ways often undetectable, by biblical textuality.

In his contribution to McConnell's collection of essays on biblical narratives, Professor Hans Frei attempts to protect biblical narratives from the encroachments of literary criticism and theory because such interests tend to dilute the particularity of texts that belong to and are finally meaningful only for a certain community. He wants them to be "insider" narratives, and he wants "insider" interpretations of them.[3] What bothers me about this argument is not its defensiveness so much or its curtailment of the authority of these texts. It is my contention that the appearance of God in narrative/textual form reveals something not only about God but also about narrativity and textuality. More than that, I think that biblical narratives reveal and have the capacity continually to reveal our actual position in narrativity and textuality. Theologically, this is not a startling thing to say. The appearance of God in any form also reveals the nature of that form and its status and function in the broader world.

The position I am taking estranges me not only from theologians who would want to preserve biblical narratives as relevant only to a particular people and their lives; it also distances me from the assumption that a sharp distinction can be made between biblical narratives, with their religious qualities or functions, on the one hand, and narratives with purely secular characteristics and roles, on the other. This assumption is fundamental, for example, to all proposals that a gap exists between "myth" and its attributes—gods appear (Northrop Frye), an ontological priority is assumed (Mikhail Bakhtin), a demand for unconditional assent is implied (Frank Kermode)—and other kinds of narratives.[4] Current narrative theory does not work with secular narrative so much as it seeks to secularize narrative. But as we have seen, all narratives, not only biblical, incorporate or lead to beliefs because all narratives contend with mystery. The appearance of God in biblical narratives neither distorts the form nor creates a separate kind of narrative; divine appearance reveals what all narrative is like, what role it plays, and what status it has in and for human life as the vestibule between language and mystery. Consequently, biblical narratives and other narratives cannot so easily be separated from one another. And now we see that this continuity arises not only from their narrative form but also from the highly textual qualities of biblical narratives. We can now inquire more fully into the nature of textuality, its standing and function in human experience.

Textuality and a Shared World

As we saw, tradition and expectation, memory and anticipation, surround any particular narrative and grant it a more general world of meaning that greatly enhances a narrative's power or resonance and meaning or implication. This arises from textuality's basic characteristic, referability. The other characteristics of textuality—stability, iterability, and past-future inclusiveness—are all specific consequences of this more basic quality. The textual is that which we can assume or to which we can refer; it provides a world we have in common.

It should immediately be clear that textuality is not to be understood in opposition to orality but rather should be understood as a certain intention or consequence of discourse generally, whether it is written or oral. Specific products only serve to make the intentions and consequences of discourse—that is, to grant a common world—unmistakable. But these intentions and consequences, the existence of a common world to which we can refer, do not depend only on those artifacts we think of when the word "text" is used—books, documents, and laws, for example. To put the matter clearly: The world to which we refer, the world we have in common, is textual.

This textual world stands both behind us and before. As already indicated, textuality provides a stable, shared past and future, memory and expectation. To it the particular and the present have complex relations. The textuality that provides a world of memory and expectation modifies and is modified by the particular and the present. The particular is modified by the textual because it is largely dependent for its meaning on its relation to a broader context of significance, yet the particular can, indeed perhaps always does, modify, however slightly, the standing of the whole by its particular contribution. The particular stands out in its particularity, in its difference, because of the text into which it cannot wholly be integrated. The particular depends upon the textual for its recognizability and intelligibility, but it also alters the text, alters tradition and expectation. In doing so it shares its particularity and becomes part of the text.

This is due to the nature of present time. The present is that aspect of time to which reference cannot be made. As St. Augustine so well pointed out, it is either not yet here or already past. The present does not stand still. I cannot refer to it, and we do not have it in common. Yet only the present exists. The future is not yet, and the past is no more. Moreover, the present is time in which the future is being exchanged for the past, when expectations are being turned into memories. Like the particular, the present has a certain primacy, reality, and power, but it is constantly confronting the text of expectation and memory.

These very general comments lead the discussion of biblical textuality past the point that biblical narratives are also texts and even past the point that textuality is always present in narrativity. The crux of the matter is that textuality is unavoidable, as unavoidable as is narrativity. A concept of scripture, as we shall see, must rest on that point. It becomes possible, even necessary, to say that we live not only in a narrative world but in a textual world as well. Since narrativity and textuality are the two characteristics of biblical material that are being stressed here, the conclusion to which we are heading is that a concept of scripture is not the imposition of something foreign upon a non-narrative, nontextual situation. Rather, a concept of scripture arises naturally from the situation in which we actually find ourselves.

While the proposal that we live in a narratively construed world may not meet general and vehement objections, the proposal that we live in a textual world, that the world we have in common is textual, will encounter that kind of response. Such a response is to be expected even when, as already has been done, care is taken to stress that this proposal is not intended to slight the reality, even in some sense the priority, of the particular and the present. The first task, therefore, is to ask why proposing the textual quality of that to which we can refer is so often an affront.

This question can be answered if we first recognize that we usually think of speech as having a higher status than writing. Speech is, we tend to think, more original and purer than writing. We are conditioned to think of texts as substitutes for, or as descended from, speech or thought, which are prior to them and preferable. Speech or thought and text are frequently opposed as spirit to letter, life to death, cargo to tender.

This tendency to view textuality as secondary to and derivative from thought and speech is a part of our philosophical heritage, finding graphic expression in Plato's reservations about writing. In the *Phaedrus*, for example, Socrates, while discussing the merits of an argument concerning love, takes up the matter of writing in relation to speaking. And he treats writing as he does painting, that is, as an imitation of something else; writing cannot stand on its own. He then goes on to say:

> ... is there not another kind of speech, or word, which shows itself to be the legitimate brother of this bastard one writing, both in the manner of its begetting and in its better and more powerful nature?
>
> PHAEDRUS.   What is this word and how is it begotten, as you say?
>
> SOCRATES.   The word which is written with intelligence in the mind of the learner, which is able to defend itself and knows to whom it should speak, and before whom to be silent.
>
> PHAEDRUS.   You mean the living and breathing word of him who knows, of which the written word may justly be called the image.
>
> SOCRATES.   Exactly.[5]

The perception that something is lost as one moves from thought or speech to writing is based in this Platonic heritage. The model is of soul and body; thoughts and speech have an originally pure existence before they are embodied in texts. This housing compromises them and the process of interpreting texts must be a freeing of the original thoughts or speech from their incarceration.

In a move dictated more by the empiricism than by the idealism of our culture, we also denigrate texts because we place them sequentially after events. That is, we posit a temporal lag between events and the texts that record them: Events occur, followed by the texts that analyze, describe, or interpret them. Furthermore, this temporal lag coincides with a loss, for events are compromised in accounts. Texts are no substitute for "being there." Interpretation of texts, then, becomes not only freeing the incarcerated thoughts that they contain but also reconstructing the events they record or entities they describe as those events and entities can be thought of as actually having happened or existed.

Idealism and empiricism, the prevailing, contrary epistemologies of our culture, also lead us, as was pointed out in the opening chapter of this study, to discount the primacy of narrative. We tend to consider narratives to be the products of two originally unconnected components: ideas and entities. These same epistemologies cause us to consider texts as secondary and derivative. We think that prior to texts there are thoughts or speech and events or entities. Texts are the consequences, the more or less inadequate substitutes for the real or true things—thoughts or speech, on the one hand, and entities and events, on the other.

Another basis for our tendency to discount textuality is our desire to be grounded in something nontextual. Texts are human products, cultural and relative, and people desire a sense of reality that is natural or absolute. In any culture people tend to think of their place as ontologically, often even geographically, central. They and the gods speak the same language, and time is measured by events in their own history. The identification of culture with ontology represses the realization that most forms of behavior are not universally shared, not natural to the species, but are limited to and characteristic of one's own group. Ethnocentrism is a consequence of grounding, of the putative temporal and spatial centrality of one's group. Texts, people assume, lack the permanence to provide this grounding, and a pre- or nontextual reality is affirmed. No matter how sophisticated we become—recognizing that we do not live in a geocentric world and that some point on our globe, such as Jerusalem, Moscow, or Chicago, is not its navel—we still assume a grounding in something "real" or nontextual. From this grounding we view texts as artificial, unnecessary, and derivative.

It may appear that biblical narratives themselves urge us to discount texts. The Bible seems to stress, no less than Plato, the primacy of speech. Genesis gets things started with a divine utterance, "Let there be light." The prophetic formula is "Thus says the Lord." The Gospel of John could hardly be more emphatic in declaring primacy for a "word" not bound by texts.

Given these several factors—that we think of texts as imprisoning thoughts and compromising events, that people need a nontextual grounding from which to view texts as discrete and relative, and that the Bible seems to stress speech—it could appear at best formidable, perhaps even quixotic, to attempt a greater appreciation of textuality. But movement toward a concept of scripture based on the characteristic of textuality, along with narrativity, requires it. At least a beginning should be made.

An initial step can be taken by remembering that biblical narratives, as we already have seen, emphasize rather than repress textuality. But there are, in addition, specific emphases on writing. For example, Yahweh speaks when he gives the law to Moses, but he also writes with his finger on both sides of the tablets. The 139th Psalm affirms that the poet's days are written in a divine book (perhaps in narrative form) before any of these days actually occur; in other words, text precedes life. And a long tradition of Jewish interpretation assumes not only that the Torah existed before the world but also that the creation of the world depended upon it. The prologue to the Gospel of John, moreover, is itself based on a text, on Genesis 1; its writer, in introducing the ministry of Jesus, goes back to the beginning not only of Creation but also the beginning of Scripture. And, turning from the past to the future, we find in Ezekiel and in the book of Revelation scrolls that relate what lies ahead. Inscribed on both sides is the summation or culmination of events. The preference of spoken to written and, then, even the denigration of writing are not so clearly a part of Jewish and Christian heritages.

The causes of our uneasiness with texts are cultural, are themselves, that is, textual. The idealist tradition in our culture causes us to stress the primacy and independence of ideas that, while conveyed in texts, have a more free and airy domain as their natural home. The text of empiricism treats facts as though they form a pre- or nontextual reality that we observe behind texts and with which we can contend. Whether we begin with the primacy of idea or of fact, we end with an uneasiness with writing.

Although it is not the principal intention or consequence of his work to do so, the contemporary French philosopher Jacques Derrida has probably done more than any other one person to draw the attention of the scholarly world to textuality and to writing. To understand the point concerning textuality most relevant in his work to this discussion, we can translate his position into the more familiar philosophical problem of time, especially the question of the relation of past and future to present time.

As I already indicated, we prefer speech to writing because of our preference for present time, which seems real when compared to the other temporal categories. Past time no longer exists, and future time is yet to come. Texts are easily associated with past and future time, for they constitute the memory of what has occurred and anticipate or prescribe what will or could occur in the future. Consequently, present time and nontextuality or speech are closely tied, and to prefer one is to prefer the other. It seems to be entirely defensible to consider present time as both real and primary; the present is the only time that we can say actually "is." But we are also aware, as St. Augustine put it so well in Book 11 of his *Confessions,* that present time is so constituted as always to be passing away. It moves so rapidly from the future into the past that it eludes grasping. In other words, present time, which appears to be so real when compared to past and future time, is highly elusive. We can say that when we refer to present time it is no longer present. When we refer to it, it is already past. If we cannot refer to present time, the temporal "reality" to which we refer is really either past or future. We refer to the present only in expectation or recall. We know and can refer to the present only in its absence.

If we turn from this discussion of time back to the question of speech and texts, we can compare speech to present time because it seems to have a reality and a primacy that texts lack. Speech is in the present and is lively. Texts seem derivative and dead in comparison. But speaking also is a rapid exchange, for the hearer, of what one expects to hear and what one has heard. Furthermore, when I attempt to understand what someone means, I wait until that person has finished. While I am attempting to understand while the person speaks, I must always be prepared for the inclusion of some item that will alter that process. I understand when the speech ends. In other words, what someone has said to me becomes a kind of text, a completed statement that belongs to past time. I understand and can refer to speech in the present only as it has become past. Anticipated speech and recalled speech are textual. Text, then, is discourse to which reference can be made.

In addition to saying that discourse to which we can refer is text, we must say that whatever our speech or writing refers to is textual. It is this dimension of textuality—referability—that allows it to provide us with a world we can share. We learn about and discuss the world to a large degree in its absence. And events, whether the smashing of an atom or a sunrise, when we refer to them, when we speak of them, have not yet occurred or already are becoming past. The reality that we have in common—that is, the reality we agree on as able to be referred to—is textual.

It is mistaken to infer, as Gerald Graff does, that for Derrida there is no reality, that there is only textuality and that texts refer only to one another. While Graff correctly observes that reality "is *always already* interpreted, *already* constructed, *already* constituted by the methodological models, paradigms, sign-systems, conventions, *epistemes* through which it is given to us," it does not follow that discourse has no relation to reality whatsoever.[6] Although we refer to reality largely in its absence, we do not therefore lack knowledge of it altogether. Traces are traces of something; absence is the absence of something. This something is so important that we tend to forget how it is that we come to refer to it, how we refer to it as it already slips from our hands. The particular and the present are real. But they become real to us, they become part of a world, by becoming textual.

People seem marked by a thirst for a firm, constant reality, for a grounding, a center, and a certainty, but they do not have a nontextual reality. They have at best a version, and that version ought not to be mistaken for something else. We find ourselves, according to this view, in a world constituted by texts. Particular texts—books and essays—are only small parts of this larger textuality in which we live; ". . . the book is not in the world," says Derrida, "but the world is in the book."[7] A relation always exists, thus, both between any text and the larger textual world of which it is a part and between a text and the textual world of its reader. As Geoffrey Hartman puts it, "To some extent it can and must be argued that we have fallen into the condition of viewing all things as texts, and even the 'thing' itself is textual."[8]

Derrida's views are so controversial because they threaten the security and authority of particular understandings of reality: scientific, philosophical, or theological. We like to repress the exchange of present for past time and of presence for text because we want a shared world grounded in a truth that is accurate or fixed, unaffected, that is, by cultural and personal perspective. Derrida's philosophy gives us a shared world that is always affected by the process of sharing it. An inescapable cultural conditioning, a personal investment, enters into all of our claims of knowing and possessing a world. We find ourselves in a textual situation that is, at best, a trace of a presence or of a particular. There is no knife sharp enough finally to cut away a free or a pure present and particular from its place within a version.

On the other hand, this does not mean that we necessarily construct a textual world for ourselves that is so unaffected by reality that it is a delusion. True, some individuals and societies may live in such world; one thinks of the ghastly distortions that dissociation from reality brought on the Jim Jones community or Nazi Germany. Our expectations and memories can and should be constantly affected by our sense of the present and particular, but we cannot claim for our texts the authority of the present or of pure presence. We live in a situation of constant exchange and inter-change of presence and text. True, we can refer only to texts, and only texts give us a common world. But we need not be imprisoned by texts, victims of them. And some texts may be able, more success-fully than others, to prepare us for or re-create a sense of the present or presence even though they themselves are either no longer or not yet. Furthermore, some texts may be able, more than others, to open us to the corrections and expansions other texts can provide.

Derrida's philosophy goes a long way toward rehabilitating tex-tuality, but his position on textuality calls for several reservations or clarifications. First, Derrida does not make textuality superior to orality. The two are always interdependent. To reduce discourse to textuality would be a distortion not only of Derrida but also of discourse. Derrida himself militates against this distortion. His em-phasis on textuality is for the purpose of righting the balance. If, at some time, textuality were overly stressed in the culture, Derrida, presumably, would come out for particularity and present time. Another reservation or clarification, one against which Derrida does not so fully protect himself, concerns the self-enclosedness of discourse, as though discourse has no referent to anything outside itself. While this understanding of discourse may be true of some structuralists and poststructuralists, it need not be insisted on. While "reality" is always becoming, by means of discourse, some-thing we can refer to and share, always becoming text, and while we cannot encounter "reality" wholly apart from the textuality of mem-ory and expectation by which it will be affected, it does not follow that textuality is all that we encounter or that textuality is unaf-fected by anything that exists or occurs. Indeed, we are constantly in present time and in particular. But the present, the no-longer-or-not-yet-textual, is always related to textuality, always being re-lated to expectation and memory. This exchange need not be a repression of, a defense against, the present and particular, al-though it often may be that. Rather, events and entities affect, alter, textuality, although some continuity of textuality—that is, some continuity between future and past—will have to be maintained if these innovations are to be intelligible and shared.

The final clarification is that textuality includes the future as well as the past. Textuality for Derrida seems to be primarily related to the past. The metaphor of trace, of impression, such as a footprint might make, has a strong indication of textuality as past related to present. But textuality is also future. There is the text of expectation, of anticipation. A meaning is projected into the future by us, and we follow it. Present time and speech are always affected by that text of anticipation. The process of discourse, then, like the process of temporality, is an exchange of the textual future for the textual past, of anticipation for memory. This process is more or less affected by present time. The common world, the world to which we can refer, is the text of expectation as well as the text of recollection. As a matter of fact, the text of the future may be more important for creating a common reference point for people who differ greatly from one another. Groups of people with much in common create unity by a common reference in the past, to textual "roots," for example. But groups, such as one finds in newer religious movements in the United States, constituted by people who differ greatly from one another in religious, ethnic, and racial backgrounds, more easily find a common reference or text in the future, in expectation.

The textuality of biblical narratives, therefore, should not be repressed. Rather, the reader should understand that these narratives are stretched between past and future. They provide texts of expectation and texts of memory. They offer, by virtue of their textuality as well as by virtue of the four-fold complexity of the narrative form, a completeness of world in which the reader can stand and to which reference can be made. While no person's or people's texts of expectation and memory are identical with, incorporated within, or completely faithful to biblical textuality, one of the dynamic interactions that occur in the reading of biblical narrative is between the memories and expectations that establish the world of the reader and those that constitute the world of biblical textuality.

Biblical textuality, for all of its particular force and its own characteristics, is intimately related to biblical narrativity. As we saw, the elements of narrative incorporate textuality to generate their particular effects. It may be possible to describe the relation between the two more exactly. The text of memory appears to be more closely tied to narrative plot and character. The text of expectation appears to be more closely tied to narrative atmosphere and tone. Narrativity cannot be construed as independent from textuality. Nor can our position be described as ever free from either.

5

Textuality and Scripture

Biblical narratives, as "highly textual," are relevant to our actual situation within a textual field. This means that a principal characteristic of biblical material, textuality, does not force the material into an artificial or special situation but relates it to the nature of our world. It is hoped that now these two principal characteristics, narrativity and textuality, have been sufficiently described to allow us to recognize in them potential for a literary doctrine of scripture.

Before we can turn to this concluding topic, however, the nature of textuality in relation to scripture must be clarified further, for the topic introduces a conflict that at this moment is quite active, one would almost say virulent. It can be described as a conflict between "writing" and "canon." After we have examined what is meant by these terms and why they stand in potential conflict with one another, we can focus on the main issue, namely, the question of a center within the textual field. The path we shall follow is between the Scylla and Charybdis of "writing" and "canon" and toward a literary concept of "scripture."

Between "Writing" and "Canon"

The characteristics of textuality discussed in the previous chapter emphasize the coherence-granting consequences of the textual world in which, as speakers and writers, hearers and readers, we find ourselves: referability, stability, and iterability. The textuality of past and future time grants a way of describing constancy in culture, our dependence upon it, and the way in which it creates and sustains discourse. Textuality reminds us that we are never wholly free from culture's specificities, never wholly individuated or disoriented, and never able to establish ourselves on some rawly natural or rational place free from text.

The consequence of textuality in granting us a common world is generally positive in nature. But our unavoidable position in the textual also has a negative side. This negative side of textuality can be indicated by the word "writing." What is meant is not the act of writing but that which has been written. The coherence-granting consequences of textuality are attacked under the banner of this term.

The term "writing" connotes something unavoidably disorienting, invasive, and unending. "Textuality" conceals these characteristics under the suggestion that texts are discrete and coherent instances of discourse. "Writing," as a more general term, breaks down the coherence and independence carried by the term "text" and opens before us a wide field of interpenetrating, competing, and often antagonistic discourses. So considered, discrete texts are dissolved into a larger field of writing, upon which they draw, in relation to which their intelligibility arises, and by which their meanings are contradicted. Speaking against particularity in the textual field, Geoffrey Hartman says, for example, "we no longer live in a world defined by certain writings having testamentary force and bending us authoritatively to their yoke. Today Old and New Testaments are simply two 'texts' in a series that is profane and endless . . . and to which, say, *Krapp's Last Tape* is just another addition."[1] There is a truth here that should be recognized: Every text, including the Bible, stands alongside thousands, even millions, of other texts, some of them competing with and others of them antagonistic to affirmations central to it, challenging, even subverting, the order of that person or group for which the text has meaning and authority. This situation of a text cannot be ignored, because, by being an instance of "writing," a text depends for its intelligibility and visibility on the field to which it is related and from which it is distinguished. We can read a text because we can read and because we read other texts from which we distinguish it. Furthermore, a text depends on the many other texts that are taken up into it, on the tradition of various interpretations of it, and on other texts influenced, positively or negatively, by it. One cannot, therefore, separate a text from this field. By being writing, a text loses independence and authority.

We must also recognize that the desire to free a text from this field of writing, like the move to a nontextual ontological grounding, can be motivated by the desire to exert power and authority and to repress, for ideological and psychological reasons, the claims of other texts. Indeed, it is difficult to dissociate the proposition of autonomous texts from associations of power and exclusion.

The conditions of "writing" are also well described by Roland Barthes. For him the containing membranes that grant the appearance of individuality and coherence to texts are incomplete, and breaks in those membranes can always be found. A particular text is woven from a plurality of signifiers that had or have places in other contexts. A text is largely constituted, therefore, of quotations without quotation marks.[2]

The negative implications of Barthes's understanding of writing for a concept of scripture have been fully drawn recently by Mark C. Taylor, especially in his book *Erring: A Postmodern A/theology*. Taylor's general purpose is to dismantle completely the sense of an authoritative self, of a coherence that favors one's own group, and the autonomy and authority of texts. "Writing" is the term that he uses to dissolve the illusion of textual self-sufficiency or self-coherence. "Writing" becomes a great leveler, revealing the lack of center in, and the interrelatedness of, all discourse. In full accord with Derrida, Taylor takes language as the mark of absence, the absence not only of God but also of the centered self, of history, and of coherence. "Writing" places us as wanderers on a centerless and endless expanse buffeted by the interplay between identity and difference, particularity and generality, contention and denial. And as wanderers, each of us cannot be sure "where he comes from, where he is, or where he is going. The impossibility of locating an unambiguous center leaves the wanderer rootless and homeless; he is forever *sans terre*."[3]

Taylor's radical position is a consequence, at least in part, of the context of power and the struggle for power that he gives to his discussion of writing. He takes the human enterprise in the modern period to be a relentless grasp for self-serving power. The overthrow of God had behind it the purpose of displacing God with a deified human subject. Since then this human subject has engaged in the policies of "mastery, utility, consumption, ownership, propriety, property, colonialism, and totalitarianism."[4] Consequently, the subject of scripture also takes on the coloration of privilege and despotism. The loss of textual authority frees signs, he says, "from restrictive borders and repressive limits," frees them now to wander "like homeless vagrants who, having lost anchor, are forever cast adrift."[5]

Although with a nonauthoritative emphasis, Taylor grants to writing, with all of its centerlessness, relativity, and lack of presence, the surprising designation of "divine milieu." That is, the presence of God is recognizable in the thoroughly kenotic situation of authority- or power-emptying that we encounter in writing. As a consequence, all writing is scripture for Taylor. That is, to understand book, text, and language as writing is to understand language as presence in absence, as, in fact, the divine milieu, "the *medium* of all presence and absence."[6]

Putting aside until later Taylor's surprising reversal, his affirmation of presence in absence and of all writing as scripture in spite of its vastness and mutually contradictory effects and competing claims, we should recognize the forceful way in which he counters the pretensions behind any erection and defense of authoritative texts, and Taylor does this with arguments influenced by Barthes and Derrida. The question is whether "writing," with its disorienting and invasive qualities, is adequate to describe our actual situation in the textual field.

The term that stands as a contrary to "writing" is "canon." While "writing" draws attention to the most generalizing and disorienting consequences of textuality, "canon" draws attention to the action of persons or groups whereby a collection of texts is established as central in the textual field. The conflict between "writing" and "canon" is by no means limited to religious or theological discussion. Indeed, the sharpest disagreements have arisen in literary studies, where there arises the need regularly to study, indeed to advocate, certain texts and to establish, both for curricular reasons and for determining competency and unity within the scholarly field, a set of texts as in one way or another normative.

It is understandable that a group, whether religious or literary, would establish, for the sake of coherence or identity, a set of texts as in some way central, even authoritative. The danger in doing so is two-fold. The first danger is the denial of the continuity that the normative texts hold with the excluded texts, even the dependence on them. The fixing of a canon creates contrast. Indeed, it is acknowledgment of a wider textual field and its power and influence that gives rise to the need for "canon" in the first place. More than that, the genuine value of excluded texts, even value judged by standards central to the "canon," can be overlooked. Finally, excluded texts may have strengths that come to light only in relation to neglected values. In other words, there is generally something exclusive and limiting about fixing a "canon." For this reason, deliberate canon-making is justifiable primarily in response to the threat of incoherence and loss of identity. Canon-making is a somewhat desperate act. The second danger is that what may have been done of historical necessity, to answer a need for coherence and identity, is taken as an ontological or rational necessity. Attributed to the selected texts is a unique value, and to neglected or rejected texts an inherent and permanent inferiority grounded in something nontextual.

"Canon" unavoidably derives connotations from its root, from one of the meanings of the Greek word that designates a standard of measure or exactitude, such as a carpenter's rule. It carries the meaning of "standard" both as something to which compliance is expected and as something applied in order to test. While the word is often used more loosely, and while one hears of "open" or flexible canons, the word carries with it the meaning of rigidity and finality. The word connotes measure or rule, and this function gives to "canon" the suggestion of permanence. One purpose of "canon" is to provide or protect coherence and identity by agreeing on a standard by which other texts can be judged. When the term is used more informally, as it is in literary studies when one speaks of the "canon" of an author's works, it may, because it has more specific meanings, confuse or exacerbate a problem that already is a difficult one, the problem of designating a center in the textual field.

It is important to recognize that in Jewish and Christian history "canon"-making is a response to stress. It is brought on by the need of a religious community to protect itself from an alien context or to alienate those within the community who appear to promulgate doctrines or behavior threatening the community's identity and coherence.[7] "Canon" is not the same as "central" or even "authoritative." Canon-making is intentionally a limited and limiting act. These qualities set "canon" in a contrary relation to the term "writing," and it may be equally inadequate for describing our actual situation in the textual field.

A. C. Sundberg points out, for example, that in the early Christian church many texts were considered religiously authoritative that were not included in the canon. Canonicity represents a second move, a designation among central texts of those that will be used to judge the standing of other texts. Sundberg suggests that the term "scripture" is a more appropriate term for the wider, less securely fixed group of texts that operated within the church to edify and instruct.[8]

"Scripture," therefore, may be a term we could think of as standing between "writing," with its emphasis on the decentering, disorienting, and often disrupting consequences of textuality, and "canon," with its suggestions of permanence, limit, and exclusiveness. It suggests a textual center that provides coherence and identity while denying neither the broader textual field on the one hand nor the need of groups under stress to clarify, from time to time, their own coherence and identity.

In order to propose "scripture" as this middle term, the topic of textual "center" must be addressed. Remembering that this topic cannot be clarified by appeals to something ontological or rational, something, that is, that one could hold to on a purely nontextual ground, we should see that the idea of a textual center, rather than arbitrary, is required. In order to clarify the need for a center we will turn to theorists of "writing," since the idea of center is not opposed by the concept of "canon."

The Need for a Textual Center

We should note, first of all, that the idea of a textual center is not absent from the works of Derrida, Barthes, and Mark C. Taylor. Although Derrida is suspicious of canons because of the ideological and psychological use of them as forms of repression and because canon can become a substitute for, or a means of, claiming some kind of ontological or rational privilege, he does not deny the necessity of a textual center. Indeed, he believes that it is impossible to avoid a center, although he is more interested in borders and peripheries than in centers and although the center is for him always instrumental or functional. "I believe," he says, "that the center is a function, not a being—a reality, but a function. And this function is absolutely indispensable."[9] We can go on to give some reasons for the indispensability of a center. For one thing, a person cannot be everywhere in the field of writing at any one time. Moreover, a person is not at any time just anywhere. Furthermore, only a part of the field is open to any one person or group of people because of differences in language, abilities, and interests. A person or a group, even a culture, can always to some degree be located in the field of writing. Since a person, group, and culture are textually limited and determined, there can be no possibility that at any one time the entire field of writing is always open to all as an undifferentiated playground. But Derrida, by calling a center indispensable, does not, bear in mind, mean a single and fixed point in the textual field. Any place open to a person, he seems to imply, can be chosen to function as center. And, we can take him further to mean, once a center is chosen it should not be elevated to permanence or defended as necessary. The center is neither a presence in the textual field nor a norm in relation to its borders.

Perhaps it is possible to elaborate Derrida's position further by exchanging spatial for temporal categories. The center can also be related to present time. Textuality provides a past and a future; it is that, in time, to which reference can be made. But past and future also have another function: They clarify present time, even though present time is never a reality with which we can identify ourselves, never a reality to be grasped. While the status of present time in Derrida is a matter open to debate—does he deny present time altogether?—it can be argued that textuality, when treated temporally rather than spatially, clarifies present time while it also keeps us from establishing present time as stable, as something to which we can refer. This means, however, that present time, while we cannot own it, is also always "when" we are.

It remains, now, to relate the moment of choice that lies behind Derrida's notion of the center as a function to this present time. It appears that for him the choice of what shall act as center is made in the present, that it is not a part of the textuality in which a choice of center is made. This means that in his work there lingers an indispensable present, a nontextual, free-floating "now" that is textually undetermined. In his insistence on the center as functional, Derrida reveals a reliance on an abstracted will freely deciding where on the textual field the center shall be. He implies that the matter of what shall serve as center is a decision the individual makes from some nontextual, nontemporal "now." Like George Meredith's comic spirit or like a bird in flight, the individual can hover over the textual terrain and settle where it will. By acknowledging the functional necessity of the center, Derrida imputes to the human will a freedom from textuality; indeed, it may be the consequence, if not the intention, of his granting alterity to writing to free, in ways similar to Jean-Paul Sartre, decision as an identifying human act. If so, Derrida admits a present that it has been his aim all along to exclude.

A similar move can be detected in Barthes. He stresses, as already has been noted, that all texts are open to the larger field of writing to which a particular text conforms, by which it is always determined, and which it plagiarizes. This means that in reading a text we are always encountering the familiar, always tied to the larger field without which the text would have no existence or intelligibility. But the pleasure of a text, to use the title of one of his books, arises from something else, from a certain play within the text caused by the gap between the familiar and the new, the general and the particular, the culture and its subversion.[10] It is neither in the one nor the other that the play and the pleasure of the play arise but in their juxtaposition. The pleasure is in the movement between them, the gaps they open as the difference between them is noticeable, and the exposure that, together, the rule and the exception create.

Barthes can be taken as saying two things here. The first, more obvious matter is that the particular, the new, the exception, is revealed by its juxtaposition with the familiar or traditional. The second matter is less obvious. Barthes reveals an interest in something nontextual that the gap between the particular and the inherited reveals. What attracts him in the text, that which has for him a particularly erotic interest, is the slit between the individual and the general. Here lies his indebtedness to Edgar Allan Poe.[11] Poe and his characters are haunted and lured by thresholds and gaps—eyes, mouths, windows, doors, other orifices as well—in order to get out of the insubstantiality of the carnal. For Barthes the carnal is the body or corpus of the writing, and it is away from it, like Poe, that he wants to go, to something behind which is not carnal. For Poe this something else, of course, is spiritual, the power of the single, originating idea from which all has descended or fallen. One is not surprised to find this Platonism in Poe (*Eureka*), but in Barthes . . . ? As Jonathan Culler puts it, Barthes "does not seek a condition *prior* to meaning but imagines one *beyond* meaning (an *après-sens*). . . ."[12]

Barthes appears to assume a textual center in his *Pleasure of the Text* and *S/Z*. First there is stress, as in all of his work, of course, on the slippage, the point of contact, between the collective and the individual, the traditional and the new, the classic and the puzzling. Barthes's exceptionalism depends upon the standard, and that standard is the textual center of a culture. In addition, Barthes suggests the scriptural in his principle of rereading. His famous parenthetical assertion, "(those who fail to reread are obliged to read the same story everywhere)," points to two kinds of repetition, one of which he prefers.[13] It is better to read something already known in a new way than to read something unknown in a familiar way. As a matter of fact, all reading can and should be rereading, since every text must include what is familiar, the already known. Rereading is not work but play, not absorption but liberation, not consumption but distancing. Rereading, it should be noted, relies on a scripture, and Barthes is well known for his own rereadings of the scripture of French literature—Racine and Balzac, for example.

If it is true that Derrida, in the moment of choosing a center, reveals a prior meaning, a nontextual, nontemporal will upon which coherence depends, and Barthes forgoes meaning for the sake of an *après-sens*, then Mark Taylor's position, dependent as it is on their work, is more radical than theirs. The question, then, is whether or not it is possible to posit, as he does, an undifferentiated field for wandering that suddenly turns from salt-flat, so to speak, to divine milieu without a particular scripture of some sort. If Taylor, in other words, does not deny authority in order to affirm a nontextual meaning prior to text, as Derrida does, or a meaning after text, as Barthes does, is it possible to deny it in order to affirm the entire textual field as scriptural, as divinely meaningful?

The simplest interpretation of Taylor's proposals is that the field of writing in which we find ourselves and on which we wander not knowing where or who we are is a field that is meaningful not to us but only to God. But Taylor seems to opt for a more modest and also more complicated theological point. To do so he draws on a central theological tradition, one that stresses that God is to be found not in the centers of power—in canon, in hierarchy, in group ascendancy—but in powerlessness, not in self-assertion but in anonymity, not in grasping but in emptying. The lineage of textual precedents that such an affirmation has behind it is clear: the Pauline celebration of the *kenosis* in Philippians 2, the appearance of the Lion of the tribe of Judah as a lamb in the Apocalypse, the tradition of ascetic Christian practice, Luther on humility, Kierkegaard on sacrifice, and Bonhoeffer on discipleship (to name only a few in this long line of texts). In other words, Taylor's affirmation has force not because he pushes his case to its logical conclusion and because he writes so well (which he does) but because his affirmation is central to the tradition. It is scriptural. Indeed, I would say that no point is more central to the New Testament than this interplay between presence and absence. Indeed, it may be possible to account for the very forms of New Testament writings themselves in this way, the interplay between the textuality of absence (epistle) and the textuality of presence (narrative).

The point to be drawn from these three positions on the relation of "writing" to coherence is that the attempt to press to an extreme the negative consequences of "writing" is an attempt that ends in affirming meaning of a very particular kind: a coherence granting will, the choice, for Derrida; a flash of naked textlessness for Barthes; and strength in weakness for Taylor. The lesson to be learned is that, even if unintended, the consequence of pressing too far the uncentered, meaningless, and undifferentiated field of writing is to have meaning appear in some kind of unexpected or nontextual way. The negative consequences of our position in a field of "writing," while needing always to be kept in mind, should not be pressed so far as to cancel them out for some positive contrary.

We end, then, with the recognition that, while no text has autonomy or complete originality but shares with other texts a common field, one marked by differences and similarities, we cannot project ourselves on this field as though on some unmarked expanse, dislocated wanderers with no beginning place, no goals, and no guiding way. This is because we cannot divest ourselves completely of continuity, coherence, or identity as individuals, groups, or a culture. A literary concept of scripture, therefore, avoids these various options: reliance on an uplifted will, free-floating in the present and choosing a functional center (Derrida); the postponement of meaning for the sake of something behind it (Barthes); and a wandering on the fields of writing as though on a vast, unordered expanse that is given a certain theological meaning by a quite specific textual tradition (Taylor).

The point to be made against these options is that any person, group, or culture is locatable in the textual field, and that location is neither wholly avoidable nor unchangeable. Stanley Fish does a good job of illuminating this role of a center in the field of writing by which we are influenced often without our awareness. We become aware of its role when we recognize that we take certain things to be important, obvious, or intelligible and others as not. So, Fish argues, in any reading situation there lies, behind or beneath both the text and the reader, a third coherence-providing influence. He calls it the "interpretive community" (Josiah Royce called it "The Community of Interpretation"). This third factor is not a group of people, as his term suggests, but a kind of textuality, a set of assumptions and beliefs operating below the level of recognition. Fish says: "Indeed, it is interpretive communities, rather than either the text or the reader, that produce meanings and are responsible for the emergence of formal features. . . . To put it another way, the claims of objectivity and subjectivity can no longer be debated because the authorizing agency, the center of interpretive authority, is at once both and neither."[14] For Fish, then, we are never in an authority-less situation. There is always an implicit, tacit text that operates in such a way as to make particular texts meaningful. This prior text is, therefore, a kind of scripture, guiding a person or group to be interested in some things and not in others, to take some matters as self-evidently true and others as not, to consider some propositions to be worth considering and others to be dismissed. This "center of interpretive authority," while it is always changing, is also always there.

This tacit scripture or text of our assumptions and beliefs stands, let us say, behind or below us, for it is so often unacknowledged. Indeed, not all will agree to its existence, arguing against Fish, no doubt, that their judgments and interpretations are free of assumptions and beliefs. Not only do we operate unaware of this scripture because we like to think of ourselves as minds free from such determinations; we are also unaware of it because, as Roland Barthes points out, we tend to think of our assumptions and beliefs not as textually but as naturally grounded. We equate our beliefs, our myths, with nature.[15] We like to deny, in other words, our textual location, our cultural determinations, and the role of assumption and belief in our daily life and scholarly work. But the more we deny restraints and directives the more determined by them we are likely to be.

This scripture or "center of interpretive authority" behind us, however, needs always to be questioned. Indeed, one could say that the educational process is, or ought to be, an increasing awareness of the unnaturalness, the non-necessity, of many assumptions and beliefs by which our analyses, interpretations, and evaluations are shaped. And the principal way in which that process is carried on is by means of a scripture that stands not behind or below but in front of or above us. When understood in this way, scripture is not exclusive or repressive but releasing and expanding. That is, it is possible to identify scripture as those texts that have authority because of their ability to challenge the assumptions and beliefs with which we address our world at those points when they are affirmed as obviously true, when they resist the need to give due consideration to propositions and possibilities contrary to them. It is by its authority that such a scripture ahead of or above us can challenge the limiting and usually self-serving motivations and consequences of a "center of interpretive authority" that has become perverse, has become prejudice.

Scripture ahead of us is the relatively stable but also always open and changing textual elevation in the field that calls us to something higher, to something granting a broader view, than the limits of the scripture behind us allow. The chief characteristic of scripture ahead of us is its ability to lead us into taking seriously texts that, for whatever self-serving reason, we might otherwise discount or ignore.

There are several ways in which scripture ahead of us does this work. One is through representation.[16] That is, scripture can promote difference. Generic, cultural, historical, ethnic, and sexual—however they are conceived, differences, the heterogeneity of the textual field, can be illuminated for us by a scripture that asks us to treat seriously various kinds of texts, kinds that differ from those that shape the interests of the reader and of his or her group.

Preservation is a second way, one closely tied to the first.[17] Scripture, while always changing, retards change that could be rash or shortsighted. Scripture lags, in changeability, behind taste and, certainly, behind fad. It is stabilizing, allowing a person or group to be more conscious about change, to recognize that this or that text no longer needs to be held as scriptural and that others should be so regarded.

Community is a third way, one closely tied to the second. A field's bibliography, to give a precise example, creates a common world for a group. While they are not, and need not be, similarly oriented to that common world, those within a community are oriented to a similar world. In this situation scripture provides the terms of initiation into that group.

Paradigm, a fourth way, is closely tied to the third.[18] Values vary in groups because of the differing interests by which groups are constituted. Scripture includes texts that represent those values and paradigms most clearly and forcefully. Such texts call a group back to values that have been neglected and project goals toward which a group is called to strive. In these various ways a scripture ahead of or above us keeps the world of a person or group from being as small or self-serving as it otherwise would become.

The authority of a scripture is based on the need for representativeness, preservation, community, and paradigms. Its authority is always to be felt as an invitation to greater complexity and catholicity. In this respect its authority complements the authority of scripture behind us. True, scripture may often become, or some may try to exchange it for, the reinforcement or legitimation of prejudice. But the role of scripture, rather than to foreclose on the textual field, is to grant a center that prevents foreclosure.

Biblical Texts and Scripture

These propositions allow the concept of scripture to appear as a necessary and desirable response to an actual situation and need. Rather than odd, artificial, and imposed, scripture is a quite (one could almost say) natural development given the situation we find ourselves in as persons in a world made meaningful in a textual as well as narrative way. A move toward a literary concept of scripture removes arbitrariness, gratuitousness, from the act of locating a textual center.

Perhaps one further step can be taken, and that is to suggest that biblical literature provides a suggestive model of what scripture ought to be like. Since no one is free from the necessity of having a scripture, biblical literature offers some suggestions as to what a set of texts that stresses the positive and reduces the negative qualities of scripture will be like.

One reason has already been given: Biblical texts reveal the phenomenon of intertextuality. This is the case not only between biblical texts and other ancient Near Eastern and otherwise non-canonical material but also between biblical texts themselves. Furthermore, biblical literature is polyphonic in its juxtaposition of literary strands within it, in its refusal to conceal or to repress varying accounts: the two Creation stories, the two versions of the rise of the monarchy or of the introduction of David to the court of Saul, and dissonance among the Gospels in the New Testament, for example. In addition, biblical texts are polyphonic in their literary forms. Indeed, there seems to be a certain formal inventiveness represented, a kind of formal explosion and diversification: proverb and narrative, lyric and law, parable and apocalypse, legend, saga, riddle, autobiography, oracle. There seems to be an insufficient generic vocabulary to cover all of the types. The variety taxes taxonomy. Finally, the historical, cultural diversity is significant. Babylonian, Egyptian, and Canaanite influences are felt, as well as the consequences of Persian, Hellenistic, and Roman cultures.

Along with all of this formal, textual, and cultural complexity there is, in biblical literature as well, a religious or theological polyphony. While this is not the occasion to discuss the matter in great detail, a broad depiction of this diversity can be given. There are at least three quite different theologies or religious orientations detectable in these texts. Perhaps access can be given to them by asking the question "Where is God in each?" One biblical answer to this question is that God is to be found in particular locations, such as in a sacred object or in a particular place or house. There is a specific form of divine presence in the world. The second answer is that God is *not* to be thought of as so particularly and predictably present, that the divine is free from such particularity and transcends forms. The third answer is that the divine is to be encountered in experience generally or in the structure and variety of the cosmos and its various creatures. The first answer could be called priestly, the second prophetic, and the third sapiential. The theologies of the priests, prophets, and sages (and the third of these was also largely the theology of the kings) are not only distinguishable from one another but also quite antagonistic, as conflicts depicted within the texts themselves among priests, prophets, and kings suggest. True, the three groups often overlap, and one cannot consider any group in complete isolation from the others. But a formal analysis of the three will reveal their differences.[19] Moreover, the variety of postbiblical religious forms and communities, of theological positions that all claim to have biblical texts as their authorities and bases, testifies to the variety of religious and theological orientations within the texts themselves.

This means that biblical literature as scripture, while it may provide a center, is itself decentering. The literary, textual, cultural, and theological diversity within the material produces a constant movement between granting certainty and subverting it. James A. Sanders comments, "It [the Bible] bears with it its own redeeming contradictions, and this is a major reason it has lasted so long and has spoken effectively to so many different historical contexts and communities."[20] As Herbert Schneidau puts it, biblical literature always has the potential of undercutting the center. The sense of it as a fixed, certain field is an illusion.[21]

It can be said, therefore, that, with whatever else it reveals, biblical literature discloses to its readers the textual situation as it should be characterized in its centered/uncenteredness. It grants and takes away particularity and coherence; it provides and subverts a world; it offers and challenges an identity. It is both separable from and open to the larger textual situation. Biblical literature not only reveals our textual situation; it also provides a model for what a scripture ought to be like.

Conclusion

It becomes possible, therefore, to propose a literary doctrine of scripture. This proposal depends on a recognition of the unavoidability of narrativity, textuality, and center. It then addresses the present theological situation in regard to a doctrine of scripture, and it ends with offering a concept of scripture to literary studies as well.

I

A literary doctrine of scripture rests, first of all, on the unavoidability of narrativity and textuality. Narrative, as we have suggested, is unavoidable because of its position between ordinary discourse and mystery.

The relation between narrative and ordinary discourse is revealed by the elements of narrative: character, plot, atmosphere, and tone. These elements of narrative cannot be separated from the characteristics of all discourse, from the need in discourse of subject (character), of predicate (plot), of the boundaries of a discourse that establish what is possible or allowed within it and what is not (atmosphere), and of discourse as a personal act (tone). The elements of narrative are more generally the marks of discourse, and, as a consequence, discourse has an incipient narrative form. This is why Roland Barthes can say that a sentence is a short narrative or narrative segment.[1]

The relation of narrative to mystery is revealed by the direction toward which the elements of narrative lead us, to the problematic, unsettled, and transcendent that we are always up against when we deal with human time, human nature, ontological conditions, and value. The elements of narrative—indeed, discourse itself—constantly secure the thresholds between our world and the mysterious at four critical areas of our experience. To change Mark C. Taylor's conclusion, then, we could say that narrative is the divine milieu in that the forms of discursive enterprises are traces of human wrestlings, as by the threshold of the Jabbok brook, with the inscrutable powers that name us not when we finally overcome them but in our constant contention.

"Narrativity," along with "textuality," counters the formlessness, the disorderliness, of "writing," for, as Mark Taylor, who is uneasy with narrative, says, narrative is "a centered structure," one he takes to be an imposition on the open plane of writing. It creates, as far as he is concerned, an illusory coherence and blinds the person to his or her actual condition as a "homeless vagrant" on an uncharted expanse.[2] The question is whether or not it is possible to describe the field of writing as free altogether of form. While it is true that narratives, like texts, are open to one another, so that there is always overlapping, interweaving, and oppositions within and between them, it is not possible completely to eliminate narrative as a form of discourse. The interplay and overlapping are between and of recognizably coherent segments of discourse. It is their coherence that allows repetition, dependence, and improvisation in the textual field to be recognized. The discursive field is an assemblage of more or less extended and identifiable, though often anonymous, instances of discourse. And as instances of discourse, they have a recognizable narrative form, however incipient that form may be.

In addition, one's position in the textual field, which, as we saw, is always to be taken into account, has an articulated or latent narrative form. As Hugh Kenner puts it, "a canon [It would be better to use the word 'scripture'] is not a list but a narrative of some intricacy, depending on places and times and opportunities."[3] That is, the role of scripture, of those texts that govern and liberate, limit and expand, grant coherence and challenge coherence, give us a world and take that world away, is in its ever-changing nature itself a story.

The unavoidability of our textual situation has been clarified with help from Derrida, although exceptions to his position and to interpretations of his position were also made. But while accepting his help on the matter of textuality, we have moved past the temptation of viewing "writing" as adequately descriptive of our textual situation toward a proposal for the nature and role of scripture, even toward its unavoidability. To do this we have also indicated that the contrary to "writing," "canon," is not adequately descriptive, because it denotes an act of determining identity and coherence relevant only to times of uncertainty or crisis.

A doctrine of scripture rests not on our need to have an orientation and identity in relation to narrative and texts but, rather, on the fact that we already and always have such a place. This is due to the assumptions and beliefs that we always have with us. These constitute a kind of narrative text; they are what Stanley Fish calls "beliefs," the "norms and values" that individuals and groups hold without realizing that they do so. There is, he says, "never a moment when one believes nothing, when consciousness is innocent of any and all categories of thought, and whatever categories of thought are operative at a given moment will serve as an undoubted ground."[4] We come prepared with "ways of thinking and seeing that inhere in social organizations," and these determine "cognitive possibilities."[5] They operate both to limit and to enable.

The role of scripture rests on a recognition of this often unrecognized narrative text of beliefs and assumptions. The acknowledgment of a scripture is simply a way of becoming conscious of that tacit text. What occurs is the process by which we find our own narratives reinforced or challenged by what we read, and this interaction produces a scripture, a body of texts in which this process goes on in a significant way. Texts that most forcefully and meaningfully address our own beliefs and assumptions will have a special authority for us as individuals and as members of groups.

In addition to this "natural" or personal authority, there is a more cultural and traditional aspect to scripture. The authority functions in such a way as to urge or even to require us to take into consideration texts that would otherwise be slighted because of their difficulty, distance, or difference from us. Scripture serves to prevent the neglect, by individuals and communities, of texts that, for self-serving reasons, they would like to neglect. This aspect to the authority of scripture counters the limiting consequences of the first, the authority that derives from the close relation that may exist between the assumptions and beliefs of a person or group and certain narrative texts. Scripture, in other words, can call attention to, rather than conceal, the larger field of writing of which it is a part.

A literary concept of scripture, therefore, is built upon three propositions. The first concerns the status, nature, and function of narrative. The principal point to make concerning narrative is its unavoidability and indispensability. The reason why narrative has these characteristics is that it structures four sets of beliefs, required responses concerning four kinds of encounters, presupposed by experience. Narrative stands, as we saw, between language and mystery. The second proposition concerns the unavoidability and indispensability of textuality. Not only is it true that narrativity depends upon, as well as produces, textuality; it is also true that the world to which we refer, the stable and understood world, is textual in nature or is inseparable from textuality. The world we share is always textual or conditioned by textuality. The third proposition concerns orientation. Again we encounter unavoidability and indispensability. Scripture provides a center we are always speaking out of; an (often unconsciously) accepted set of beliefs, assumptions, and interests; and a center ahead of us that both confirms our own identity and coherence and challenges them, providing access to a more inclusive and complex textual world.

II

We may now ask what contribution these literary interests—narrativity, textuality, and center—make to a religious or theological concept of scripture. Answering this question depends, first of all, on an indication that religious or theological concepts of scripture need help. This should not be a surprise, given the tendencies of our culture, which were described earlier (especially in the first and fourth chapters), to discount narrativity and textuality. Before asking what relevance literary interests have to a theological under-

standing of scripture, we should look, however briefly, at the standing doctrines of scripture have in recent theology.

The task of determining the standing of scripture in recent theology is made much lighter than it otherwise would be by David
Kelsey's excellent work on this question. He demonstrates convincingly that theologians, however much they differ from one another
in other ways, share a tendency to discount scripture. He argues
that such diverse theologians as Benjamin Warfield, Karl Barth,
Paul Tillich, and Rudolf Bultmann acknowledge sacred writ not
because of its characteristics but because of its theological function.[6]
While one would expect Protestant theologians to advocate strong
doctrines of scripture, given the importance of sacred writ for the
Reformers, their understandings of scripture are derived from
their theological interests and not vice versa.

Kelsey attributes the lack of a strong concept of scripture in
Protestant theology to its functional status as supporting theological interests based elsewhere. "Theologians' decisions about how to
use scripture," he says, "like their decisions about how to *construe*
the scripture they use, are determined by decisions that are literally
pre-text, i.e., logically prior to any attention to any particular text
taken as authority for any particular theological proposal."[7] Because the reason for considering the Bible to be scripture comes
from theological interests within the theologian's own work, authority is conferred upon the Bible by something thought to be
nontextual: a system of doctrine for Warfield, divine intention for
Barth, a network of religious symbols for Tillich, or instances of
authentic existence for Bultmann. Kelsey concludes that the status
of scripture in Protestant theology and the role of scripture in the
work of particular theologians are occasioned by individually ad-
vanced "policy decisions" more than by some generally shared understanding of why and how biblical texts can be taken as sacred.

We should not be surprised by this state of affairs. In our culture,
the Bible, like any text, will readily be assigned a functional role
because of how we tend to view textuality. Texts, we tend to think,
have a derivative status granted by the functions they perform.
Texts are considered helpful but dispensable, and they derive their
importance from something else: the ideas or the events that can be
extracted or reconstructed from them.

The insubstantial doctrine of scripture in contemporary theology
is also due to the low regard in our culture for narrative discourse.
This form also projects the interests of theologians to facts and be-

liefs outside and prior to the text. As Hans Frei points out, this
attitude can be found both in conservative and liberal understandings of the Bible. In conservative views biblical narratives yield to a
divine history, of which the "history" presented by the biblical stories
themselves is only a minor part. The real narrative is the story of
divine intentions from Creation to the present day. Liberal Christianity, with its uneasiness regarding the unenlightened view of themselves and of the world with which people who produced biblical
narratives lived, abstracts the meaning and value of the narratives
from their settings; the Bible becomes a beloved, yet ultimately dispensable, tool for those matters of value it makes available. What
Frei calls "the eclipse of Biblical narrative" results from an agreement across the spectrum of theological opinion that interpretation
is a matter "of fitting the biblical story into another world with another story" rather than respecting the integrity of the biblical narratives themselves.[8]

The pervasively narrative form of biblical literature conspires,
for reasons discussed in the first chapter, with its textual nature
(Chapter 4) to diminish its stature in our culture. We tend to think
of narrative as an uneasy compound that wants to be broken down
into its original elements, namely, historical facts and the ideas or
beliefs of authors. As Frei puts it, "To close the gap between the
words of narrative and the 'real' meaning, one had to appeal to one
or more of the following: historical occurrences; the mind of the
author as distinct from his words; ideas independent of both, as
well as of the words of the text. In all three cases, the meaning is the
subject matter as distinct from the words."[9] Whatever meaning and
value biblical narratives may have in such views tend to derive from
something prenarrative as well as pretextual. Let us look briefly at
the three options cited by Frei.

Biblical scholarship has as one of its objects the reconstruction of
a coherent history behind the biblical text. When augmented by
theological interests, this history becomes a series of God's mighty
acts, a *Heilsgeschichte*. The validating theological ground of biblical
narrative is a sequence of events behind the texts that, in occurring,
created particular responses. It is to this series of events and responses to them, rather than to the drama of biblical narratives
themselves, that Bernhard Anderson refers by the title of his book
The Unfolding Drama of the Bible.[10] Liberal and conservative biblical
scholarship, although motivated theologically in differing ways,
agree that biblical narratives derive their religious meaning from

something behind them, from a series of events, from a history it is the task of the biblical scholar to reconstruct.

Another way of moving behind the text to something pretextual is, according to Frei, to focus on the attitudes or ideas of the authors rather than on the events the texts depict. An interesting example is provided by C. H. Dodd, whose principal interest is in the "genius" of biblical authors. Dodd calls attention to that "quality" of the writings that reveals the spiritual insights or attitudes of their authors. This quality provides a range of vision or an intensity and conviction of attitude in which the reader can participate: "Their words convey a personal experience of reality, and our aim is to participate in it, rather than merely to assess the logic of their arguments. If they can make us do that in any measure, then their authority has established itself. It is the only sort of authority they need claim."[11] The model, unabashedly used by Dodd, is of great artists like Dante and Shakespeare, and of a Coleridgean theory of the imagination. Genius has its own numinous validity and power: "In almost all parts of the Bible we can feel ourselves in touch with religious personalities, some of them displaying exceptional inspiration, all of them men of insight and sincerity."[12] Dodd finds not only the form of biblical material a partial barrier to his desired goal; he even thinks that words conceal genius as much as reveal it. That which grants the Bible value lies not only prior to text and narrative; it lies prior to language.

If not for the sake of a sequence of events or the genius of authors, one can look behind or beyond biblical narratives for an idea or reality, as Frei puts it, that is finally independent of events, the intentions of authors, or the words of the text. Karl Barth does this by preferring word-events to texts. One word-event is proclamation, and it stands behind and validates the texts; the Bible is "proclamation in writing."[13] It should be noted that Barth goes a long way toward recognizing the authority of the Bible as text; textuality results in an objectivity and permanence that keep the Church from engaging in a conversation only with itself. By being fixed in writing, the proclamation gains authority; "it is upon the written nature of the canon, upon its character as *scriptura sacra,* that its autonomy and independence hang, and therefore its free power toward the Church, and therefore the living nature of the succession."[14] But the text is transitional for Barth. It stands between the word-event that precedes it and the word-event, the proclamation, to which it gives rise. Barth calls the Bible an "attestation" to the original event; "to attest means to point in a definite direction beyond oneself to something else."[15] Scripture is, for Barth, a rather elusive middle term, "a medium" between two moments free from narrative and text. While it is an indispensable middle point, it has more a derived or transitional position than a substantial or determining one. It defers to and creates unity between the event that lies behind it and the event that lies in front of it. And it receives its authority from that composite "word."

Some recent understandings of scripture appear to take textuality more seriously. For example, David Tracy introduces a textual dimension to biblical authority by using the cultural and literary category of "classic." His use of that term places Tracy in a tradition of Longinian or quality criticism, which has its strongest modern spokesman in Matthew Arnold. A literary classic, according to Tracy, is a text that has the power or authority to challenge and transform the reader's "horizon of understanding."[16] A classic conveys "a reality we cannot but name truth," and reading it becomes an "event":[17] "My finite status as this historical subject is now confronted with the classic and its claim upon me: a claim that transcends any context from my preunderstanding that I try to impose upon it, a claim that can shock me with the insight into my finitude, a claim that will interpret me even as I struggle to interpret it."[18] The mark of a *religious* classic is its ability to convey the universal in the particular. It grants disclosure of the whole. Furthermore, the religious classic reveals that the whole is personal, that it is like a "who."[19] A religious classic opens the reader to the truth that the conditions of life by which we are contained ultimately possess a personal quality.

Although Tracy's use of the term "classic" appears to place textuality and literary forms in a central and determining position, he grants texts the status of "classic" not because of their literary properties but because of something outside them. The quality resides in events that are pretextual and are depicted in or conveyed by the text. In the New Testament, he says, "we find the event, the person, the story, and the images of the Christian classic codified in a diversity of genres, symbols, concepts, images, doctrines, each expressing with some degree of adequacy the meaning and truth of that decisive event."[20] The "classic" itself should not be identified with the text.

Furthermore, like all theorists in the Longinian mode, Tracy is not primarily concerned about genre. Consequently, he does not say how a certain genre, such as narrative, is able to possess the quality or produce the experience that he associates with encountering a classic. The New Testament texts, rather than being themselves classics, are "responses of both faith and imagination to the classic event of Jesus Christ."[21] The ability of the text to convey both the "classic event" and responses to it has something to do with genre, but the question of that relationship is not central to Tracy's project. Although he says that "narrative alone provides us with some fuller way to order and unify our actual lived experience with its tensions and surprises, its reversals and triumphs, its experience through memory of the past and, through anticipation and hope, of a future in the tensed unity of the ever-vanishing now of the present and its possibly illusory sense of sequence,"[22] he grants narrative a derivative and functional status. First there is the event, then the proclamation, and then the descent (he uses the word "submerge")[23] into the story form. The Gospels, for example, are first of all responses to classic events, and Tracy does not tell us how narrative texts make these events available to the reader or how they themselves possess classic quality. It appears that Tracy considers narratives to resonate, like tuning forks, to the quality of the events that gave rise to them. The vibration, then, continues through what seems a chronological progression from event to proclamation to narrative to symbol-image and to reflective thought. Tracy's Longinian method, while drawing on a distinguished literary tradition, helps us little in the task of appreciating more highly the nature of narrative texts and their contribution to the category of scripture because the method delineates a quality not only shared by many cultural and literary forms but finally independent of them.

Interesting as these theological understandings of scripture may be, they are not built on a high evaluation of narrative and writing. This is due to reasons already elaborated, to the modern tendency to disparage both narrative and textuality, to see them as derivative. Thoughts and events, beliefs and facts, we tend to assume, antedate narrative and text. We are fascinated by and seek to establish our identity on a non-narrative, nontextual reality, and we consider narrative texts to be prisons where facts and ideas are kept and from which they must be freed.

A concept of scripture built upon the characteristics of narrativity and textuality will not think it possible to begin with some non-narrative or nontextual ground, some set of ideas and beliefs or some reconstructed sequence of historical "facts." It will not assume that the standing of biblical texts is derived from something else, the events behind them or a system of doctrine that they yield. The history of Israel has authority because of the texts; the "Christ event" is an aspect of narrative texts and not something free from them.

Moreover, a literary concept of scripture will stress that narrativity and textuality, in addition to being ultimate and not penultimate characteristics, are unavoidable. This means it is not possible to assume that the characteristics of narrativity and textuality are matters of choice. It is not as though a person or a group can have identity and coherence in a nontextual, non-narrative way. Those with a concept of scripture are not odd among the world's population by being oriented to or by a set of narrative texts. On the contrary, all people, if they have ongoing lives, are thus oriented. People with a literary concept of scripture are aware that their place in a world is always structured and conditioned by narrativity and textuality.

This point needs to be stressed because it contradicts what seems to be the obvious and incontrovertible situation. That situation is nicely described by Tom Paine's *Age of Reason*. For Paine it seems utterly reasonable to contrast two kinds of authority. The one is the authority of a book, of the Bible, with all the specificity and limitations of cultural origins and priestly interpretations. On the other side is the authority of Reason and the Created Order, unencumbered by traditions, open to all, and limitless in scope. Once Paine sets up the options in this way—derivative and limited text and primary and open natural order—the choice is obvious. The reasonable reader will readily concur in Paine's decision: "The Word of God is the Creation we behold."[24] Why not choose the natural order and the power of the mind with all the open possibilities they hold over against a text that is the product of relatively few people in a relatively limited cultural and historical period?

The doctrines of scripture discussed above have no answer for this except to say that institutional or communal loyalty, an idiosyncratic interest in tradition and its texts, or a distrust of nature and reason force them to choose the admittedly more confined and derivative choice, the Bible. Moreover, they would say, if pressed, that they are not primarily oriented to text but move beyond or behind it to a set of ideas or a set of real events, so that they end up having the reasonable and the real that Paine's other choice offers even though they begin with text, as Paine does not.

A literary concept of scripture, with its assumption that narrativity and textuality are unavoidable, will not enter this debate, because of the mistaken assumption shared by all parties in it that narrativity and textuality are derivative, secondary, and optional characteristics of one's identity and orientation. A literary concept of scripture assumes that there is no reality/text or world/narrative choice to make. We have a world or are in a world structured by beliefs that stand as responses to four kinds of unavoidable mysteries. And we have a world or are in a world because we can refer to it, because it is stable, iterable, or textual. There is no time or place where we encounter the new, the individual, or the present apart from narrative and text. It would be as though we could choose not to have a future or a past and live only in the present or as though we could get up in the morning with no beliefs whatsoever about what to expect and not to expect, what people are like, whether our actions or events around us make any difference at all, or what is valuable or worthy of our attention.

This situation also clarifies the role of scripture, of that in the narrative/textual situation that grants and challenges continuity, coherence, and identity. We always are somewhere in that field, but that position always is changing, not only due to the interplay between continuity and innovation, the general and the particular, or the past-future and present time, but also due to the interplay between the texts that grant us a position and the larger textual situation that challenges its distinctiveness or adequacy. A literary doctrine of scripture, rather than adding something dispensable to theological interests, introduces theological interests into the midst of an actual situation and grants to its debates a significant cultural role.

III

It may also be possible to propose a doctrine of scripture to literary studies as an acceptable alternative between the Scylla of "writing" and the Charybdis of "canon." The present discussions hold out the rather unacceptable alternatives of a field too determined by special interests and a field too incoherent to allow for judgments concerning the relative importance of various texts or to establish identity-granting boundaries of interest and expertise. The term "scripture" may stand as a possible alternative to these options.

Its adoption, in addition, could draw attention to the roles relative to mystery and value that I have assigned narrative and text. It means a recognition that no gap can be opened between religious and secular narratives, that all narratives operate in relation to belief, and that all arise from the relation of language to mystery. And it means that any and many texts form and articulate our values and assumptions just as various texts may serve to provide or urge us toward greater complexity and catholicity.

In a recent essay on the subject, Frank Kermode calls for a view of authority in literary studies, of a textual center, that is freer and more flexible than the term "canon" allows.[25] It is a matter with which he has struggled for over a decade. Earlier he addressed the topic of the "classic" as a kind of text that is "more or less immediately relevant and available" to the modern, or at least is vulnerable to "strategies of accommodation."[26] He depends (perhaps too heavily) on T. S. Eliot, but he has in mind the problem of relating permanence or continuity to change. He says, "one may speak of the text as a system of signifiers which always shows a surplus after meeting any particular restricted reading."[27] The position Kermode takes may, however, be overly on the side of "canon," because he seems to hold out for a set of permanently fixed texts that are capable of changing and various interpretations. He is vulnerable to the challenge of Jane Tompkins when, in exposing the partisan interests that effect "the establishment of a classic author," she charges that "the literary works that now make up the canon do so because the groups that have an investment in them are culturally the most influential."[28] She calls for a more flexible situation, one open to the interplay of interests and values resulting in a more open and changing "canon." She would agree, it seems to me, with George Steiner when he says that "constructs of the 'classic' or the 'canonic' can never be anything but more or less persuasive, more or less comprehensive, more or less consequent descriptions of this or that process of preference."[29] The center is designated by taste, by, more accurately, belief and conviction, and that which constitutes the center varies not so much because tastes and convictions vary as because that which we take it important to have opinions and convictions about varies.

Perhaps a better word than "canon" is scripture, therefore, since it has the more open quality for which Tompkins calls—open, that is, to displacements within the set of texts itself. And this is always a process. Since the field will always have a center, if it is to be coherent, it is always involved in a rather specific exercise of exchanging some texts for others, of raising the status of neglected texts, and of challenging the hegemony of others. In any case, change occurs not only in the interpretations of texts but in that collection of texts that are given the special attention which that field of inquiry is capable of giving them.

The attention that literary studies gives to narrative texts need not be moral and religious, even though the texts with which its practitioners deal are never innocent in these respects. Literary studies and religious studies, although they both deal with narrative texts, are finally attentive to differing things. Religious studies are oriented primarily to the mysteries to which narrative leads and to the beliefs that particular narratives contain concerning these mysteries. Religious studies are more directly concerned with the beliefs that the "scriptures" behind and ahead of us confirm or project. Literary studies are more attentive to the "poetics" of narrative texts, to the ways in which they are made and the dependence on other narrative texts those characteristics reveal. While no clear line can be drawn between "sacred" and "secular" scripture, legitimate differences in scholarly interest and method can be maintained.

Notes

Chapter 1

1. Hayden White, "The Value of Narrativity in the Representation of Reality," *Critical Inquiry*, vol. 7, no. 1, p. 5.

2. Ferdinand de Saussure, *Course in General Linguistics*, ed. Charles Bally and Albert Sechehaye, trans. Wade Raskin (New York: Philosophical Library, 1959).

3. Barbara Hardy, "An Approach Through Narrative," in *Towards a Poetics of Fiction*, ed. Mark Spilka (Bloomington: Indiana University Press, 1977), p. 31.

4. Charles Percy Snow, *The Two Cultures and the Scientific Revolution* (Cambridge, England: Cambridge University Press, 1959).

5. Frank Kermode, *The Sense of an Ending: Studies in the Theory of Fiction* (New York: Oxford University Press, 1966).

6. Seymour Chatman, *Story and Discourse: Narrative Structure in Fiction and Film* (Ithaca: Cornell University Press, 1978); Gérard Genette, *Narrative Discourse: An Essay in Method*, trans. Jane E. Lewin (Ithaca: Cornell University Press, 1980); Günther Müller, *Morphologishe Poetik: Gesammelte Aufsätze* (Tubingen: Max Niemeyer Verlag, 1974); and Victor Erlich, *Russian Formalism: History-Doctrine* ('S-Gravenhage: Mouton and Company, 1955), pp. 209–11.

7. See Paul Ricoeur, *Time and Narrative*, vol. 1 and 2, trans. Kathleen McLaughlin and David Pellauer (Chicago: University of Chicago Press, 1984 and 1985). A similar point is made about narrative by Robert Scholes

and Robert Kellogg in their book *The Nature of Narrative* (New York: Oxford University Press, 1966) when they distinguish an empirical from a fictional pole in narrative. However, they judge these two finally not as two sides of a single whole but as inherently separated. Hence, narratives that combine aspects of both are "inclining always to break down into [their] constituent elements" (p. 15).

8. Stephen Crites, "The Narrative Quality of Experience," *Journal of the American Academy of Religion*, vol. 39, no. 3 (September 1971), pp. 291–311.

9. Reynolds Price, *A Palpable God* (New York: Atheneum, 1978), p. 3.

10. Roy Schafer, "Narrative in the Psychoanalytic Dialogue," *Critical Inquiry*, vol. 7, no. 1 (Autumn 1980), p. 35; and James Hillman, "The Fiction of Case History: A Round," in *Religion as Story*, ed. James Wiggins (New York: Harper and Row, 1975), pp. 123–74.

11. Scholes and Kellogg, *The Nature of Narrative*, p. 104.

12. Ibid., pp. 238–39.

13. See Jonathan Culler, "Fabula and Sjuzhet in the Analysis of Narrative," *Poetics Today*, vol. 1, no. 3 (Spring 1980), pp. 27–37.

14. For a more complete presentation of this theory of narrative as a system constituted by four elements, see my *Narrative Elements and Religious Meaning* (Philadelphia: Fortress Press, 1975).

15. Chatman, *Story and Discourse*, p. 137.

16. For a more complete presentation of this theory of narrative time, see my *Modern Fiction and Human Time: An Essay in Narrative and Belief* (Tampa: University of South Florida Press, 1985).

17. Chatman, *Story and Discourse*, p. 264.

18. Alasdair MacIntyre, *After Virtue* (Notre Dame: University of Notre Dame Press, 1984), p. 218. Because of his philosophical interest in ethics and anthropology, MacIntyre assumes character to be the center of narrative, and he defines the standing of character more in moral than (as I later shall) spiritual terms.

19. See, e.g., Rudolf Otto, *The Idea of the Holy*, trans. John W. Harvey (New York: Oxford University Press, 1958).

20. MacIntyre, *After Virtue*, pp. 211–12.

21. Roland Barthes, "An Introduction to the Structural Analysis of Literature," trans. Lionel Duisit, in *New Literary History*, vol. 6, no. 2 (Winter 1975), p. 241. See also *Image-Music-Text*, trans. Stephen Heath (Glasgow: William Collins Sons and Co., 1977), pp. 83–84.

22. MacIntyre, *After Virtue*, p. 211.

23. Barbara Herrnstein Smith, *On the Margins of Discourse: The Relation of Literature to Language* (Chicago: University of Chicago Press, 1978), p. 132. I do not, however, agree in every respect with her argument that fictive narratives are imitations of what she calls "natural" narratives. These two roles of narrative are separated into distinct kinds of discourse primarily by a period, as I said earlier, shaped by an epistemological dualism.

Chapter 2

1. Readers with theological as well as literary interests should bear in mind the point that the appearance of God in any form reveals something not only about God but also about the form in which God appears. See John MacQuarrie, *Principles of Christian Theology* (New York: Charles Scribner's Sons, 1977), pp. 84–103.

2. David Rhoads and Donald Michie, *Mark as Story: An Introduction to the Narrative of a Gospel* (Philadelphia: Fortress Press, 1982), p. 36. The notes of the book also provide a helpful bibliography for literary studies of biblical narrative, particularly of the Gospels.

3. Norman R. Petersen, " 'Point of View' in Mark's Narrative," in *Semeia 12: The Poetics of Faith: Essays Offered to Amos Niven Wilder*, ed. William A. Beardslee (Missoula, MT: Scholars Press, 1978), pp. 116–17.

4. Rhoads and Mitchie, *Mark as Story*, p. 40.

5. Ibid., p. 61.

6. For a semiotic study of place names in the Gospels, see Louis Marin, *The Semiotics of the Passion Narrative: Topics and Figures* (Pittsburgh: Pickwick Press, 1980), especially pp. 23–91.

7. Rhoads and Michie, *Mark as Story*, p. 65.

8. "By definition we could say that the narrator [of the parables] sets aside his own personality in order to have a voice other than his own, that is unless he causes the voice which bestows meaning to be heard rightly by disappearing within it while his listeners lose themselves in the 'naked' hearing. *The parable is that moment in which the word belongs to no one.*" *Signs and Parables: Semiotics and Gospel Texts*. Papers of the Entrevernes Group (Pittsburgh: Pickwick Press, 1978), p. 256.

9. "The place from which Jesus speaks is an elsewhere which is not to be identified with the space where the old values are ordered" (A. J. Greimas, "Postface," in Ibid., p. 309).

Chapter 3

1. Rodolphe Gasché, *The Tain of the Mirror: Derrida and the Philosophy of Reflection* (Cambridge: Harvard University Press, 1986), p. 122.

2. John Vickery, ed., *Myth and Literature: Contemporary Theory and Practice* (Lincoln: University of Nebraska Press, 1966), p. x.

3. Ernst Cassirer, *The Philosophy of Symbolic Forms*, vol. 2, "Mythical Thought," trans. Ralph Manheim (New Haven: Yale University Press, 1955), p. 74. See Philip Wheelwright, "Notes on Mythopoeia," in Vickery,

Myth and Literature, pp. 64–65. See also his *Burning Fountain* (Bloomington: Indiana University Press, 1954).

4. See Frederick J. Hoffman, *Freudianism and the Literary Mind* (Baton Rouge: Louisiana State University Press, 1945); Louis Fraiberg, *Psychoanalysis and American Literary Criticism* (Detroit: Wayne State University Press, 1960); and Carl Jung, "Psychology and Literature," in *Modern Man in Search of a Soul* (New York: Harcourt, Brace, 1934), pp. 152–72.

5. Philip Rahv, "The Myth and the Powerhouse," in Vickery, *Myth and Literature,* p. 111.

6. Norman N. Holland, *The Dynamics of Literary Response* (New York: Oxford University Press, 1968), p. 246.

7. Ibid., p. 248.

8. Joseph Campbell, *The Hero With a Thousand Faces* (New York: Meridian Books, 1956), p. 10.

9. Wallace Douglas, "The Meaning of 'Myth' in Modern Criticism," *Modern Philology* (May 1953), p. 234.

10. Richmond Hathorn, *Tragedy, Myth, and Mystery* (Bloomington: Indiana University Press, 1962), p. 27.

11. Campbell, *The Hero With a Thousand Faces,* pp. 30–35.

12. Paul Ricoeur, *Time and Narrative,* vol. 1, trans. Kathleen McLaughlin and David Pellauer (Chicago: University of Chicago Press, 1985), p. 67.

13. Northrop Frye, *The Great Code: The Bible and Literature* (New York: Harcourt Brace Jovanovich, 1982), p. 46.

14. Northrop Frye, *The Anatomy of Criticism* (New York: Atheneum, 1966), pp.158–239, and *The Secular Scripture: A Study of the Structure of Romance* (Cambridge: Harvard University Press, 1976), p. 97.

15. Frye, *The Great Code,* p. 80.

16. Ibid., p. 192.

17. Mircea Eliade, *Cosmos and History: The Myth of the Eternal Return,* trans. Willard R. Trask (New York: Harper and Row, 1959), p. 88. For a more complete study of Eliade's theory of narrative time, see my *Modern Fiction and Human Time: An Essay in Narrative and Belief* (Tampa: University of South Florida Press, 1985), pp. 58–70.

18. Mircea Eliade, *Myth and Reality,* trans. Willard R. Trask (New York: Harper and Row, 1963), p. 192.

19. William Righter, *Myth and Literature* (London: Routledge and Kegan Paul, 1975), p. 126.

20. Eric Gould, *Mythical Intentions in Modern Literature* (Princeton: Princeton University Press, 1981), p. 39.

21. Ibid., pp. 115–16.

22. For a substantial introduction, see Michael Lane, ed., *Introduction to Structuralism* (New York: Basic Books, 1970); and Jonathan Culler, *Structuralist Poetics: Structuralism, Linguistics and the Study of Literature* (Ithaca: Cornell University Press, 1975).

23. Ferdinand de Saussure, *Course in General Linguistics,* ed. Charles Balley and Albert Sechehaye, trans. Wade Raskin (New York: Philosophical Library, 1959).

24. Tzvetan Todorov, "Structuralism and Literature," in *Approaches to Poetics: Selected Papers from the English Institute,* ed. Seymour Chatman (New York: Columbia University Press, 1973), p. 155.

25. Jonathan Culler, *Structuralist Poetics,* p. 77. See also Tzvetan Todorov, *The Poetics of Prose,* trans. Richard Howard (Ithaca: Cornell University Press, 1977), p. 223.

26. Vladimir Propp, *Morphology of the Folktale,* trans. Laurence Scott (Bloomington: Indiana University Press, 1958), p. 6.

27. Elder Olson, *Tragedy and the Theory of Drama* (Detroit: Wayne State University Press, 1961), p. 79.

28. Roland Barthes, *Image-Music-Text,* trans. Stephen Heath (Glasgow: William Collins Sons and Company, 1977), pp. 81–84.

29. Ibid., pp. 127–28.

30. A. J. Greimas and F. Rastier, "The Interaction of Semiotic Constraints," *Yale French Studies,* no. 41 (1968), pp. 86–105.

31. Fredric Jameson, *The Political Unconscious: Narrative as a Socially Symbolic Act* (Ithaca: Cornell University Press, 1981), p. 121.

32. A. J. Greimas, *Structural Semantics: An Attempt at a Method,* trans. Daniele McDowell et al., Introduction by Ronald Schleifer (Lincoln: University of Nebraska Press, 1983), p. 121.

33. Ibid., pp. 171–72.

34. Ibid., pp. 206–7.

35. Noam Chomsky, *Aspects of the Theory of Syntax* (Cambridge: MIT Press, 1965), p. 4.

36. Robert C. Culley, *Studies in the Structure of Hebrew Narrative* (Philadelphia: Fortress Press, 1976), p. 23. For other studies of structuralist analysis of biblical narrative, see Alfred M. Johnson, ed., *Structuralism and Biblical Hermeneutics* (Pittsburgh: Pickwick Press, 1979); Robert M. Polzin, *Biblical Structuralism: Method and Subjectivity in the Study of Ancient Texts* (Philadelphia: Fortress Press, 1977); and Daniel Patte, *What is Structural Exegesis?* (Philadelphia: Fortress Press, 1976).

37. E. D. Hirsch, *Validity in Interpretation* (New Haven: Yale University Press, 1967). For an introduction to this current of scholarship, see Edgar V. McKnight, *Meaning in Texts: The Historical Shaping of a Narrative Hermeneutics* (Philadelphia: Fortress Press, 1978), pp. 66ff.

38. Richard E. Palmer, *Hermeneutics: Interpretation Theory in Schleiermacher, Dilthey, Heidegger, and Gadamer* (Evanston: Northwestern University Press, 1969), p. 244.

39. Hans-Georg Gadamer, *Truth and Method* (New York: Seabury Press, 1975), p. 401.

40. Ibid., p. 431.

41. Ibid., p. 62.

42. Ibid., p. 164.

43. Paul Ricoeur, *Fallible Man: Philosophy of the Will*, trans. Charles Kelbley (Chicago: Henry Regnery Co., 1965), pp. xix–xx.

44. Paul Ricoeur, *The Conflict of Interpretation*, ed. Don Ihde (Evanston: Northwestern University Press, 1974), pp. 21, 117, 120, 171, 175, 325, and 333.

45. Ibid., p. 298.

46. Paul Ricoeur, *The Rule of Metaphor: Multidisciplinary Studies of the Creation of Meaning in Language*, trans. Robert Czerny (Toronto: University of Toronto Press, 1975), p. 229.

47. Ibid., pp. 156–57. See also my article "Paul Ricoeur and the Hermeneutics of Metaphor," *Christianity and Literature*, vol. 28, no. 2 (Winter 1979), pp. 49–51.

48. Paul Ricoeur, *Time and Narrative*, vol. 1, trans. Kathleen McLaughlin and David Pellauer (Chicago: University of Chicago Press, 1984), pp. 3 and 52.

49. Ibid., pp. 66–67 and 207.

50. Ibid., p. 41.

51. Ibid., pp. 77–79.

52. Martin Heidegger, *On Time and Being*, trans. Joan Stambaugh (New York: Harper and Row, 1972), pp. 1–24.

53. Karl Mannheim, *Ideology and Utopia: An Introduction to the Sociology of Knowledge* (New York: Harcourt Brace and Co., 1954). This point also appears in Ricoeur's essay "The Biblical Worldview and Philosophy," *NICM Journal for Jews and Christians in Higher Education* (Summer 1981), pp. 91–112, especially pp. 109–11. He says, ". . . ideology has a . . . basic function, which is to integrate community through a whole range of symbolic procedures (commemoration of founding events, social ritual, etc.) . . . According to this foundational role an ideology is a system of images or symbols which *preserves* the identity of the group and of its members against external or internal threats" (p. 109). ". . . Utopias keep open alternatives to this given order" (p. 110).

54. Meir Sternberg, *The Poetics of Biblical Narrative: Ideological Literature and the Drama of Reading* (Bloomington: Indiana University Press, 1985), p. 15.

55. Ibid., p. 9.

56. Ibid., p. 73.

57. Eric Auerbach, *Mimesis: The Representation of Reality in Western Literature*, trans. Willard R. Trask (Princeton: Princeton University Press, 1953), p. 6.

58. James Barr, *The Semantics of Biblical Language* (Oxford: Oxford University Press, 1961), pp. 8–20.

59. Thorlief Boman, *Hebrew Thought Compared with Greek,* trans. Jules L. Moreau (London: SCM Press, 1960).

60. Hans Jonas, "The Nobility of Sight," in *The Phenomenon of Life: Toward a Philosophical Biology* (New York: Harper and Row, 1966), pp. 135–52.

61. Sternberg, *The Poetics of Biblical Narrative,* p. 46.

62. Ibid., p. 184.

63. Robert Alter, *The Art of Biblical Narrative* (New York: Basic Books, 1981), pp. 51 and 95.

64. Ibid., pp. 70–73.

65. Ibid., pp. 140–54.

66. Frank Kermode, *The Genesis of Secrecy: On the Interpretation of Narrative* (Cambridge: Harvard University Press, 1979), pp. 1–21.

67. Ibid., pp. 125–45.

68. Ibid., pp. 75–99.

Chapter 4

1. It is because Meir Sternberg is attentive to what I am calling "tone" in narrative that he can draw attention, as the subtitle to his *Poetics of Biblical Narrative* makes clear, to "The Drama of Reading." Indeed, it can be said that so-called reader-response theory is attentive primarily to the textuality of tone as that ahead of the reader and which the reader follows.

2. Frank McConnell, ed., *The Bible and the Narrative Tradition* (New York: Oxford University Press, 1986), p. 14.

3. Hans W. Frei, "The 'Literal Reading' of Biblical Narrative in the Christian Tradition: Does It Stretch or Will It Break?," in Ibid., pp. 36–77.

4. See Northrop Frye, *Anatomy of Criticism* (New York: Atheneum, 1966), p. 33; Mikhail M. Bakhtin, *The Dialogic Imagination: Four Essays,* trans. Caryl Emerson and Michael Holquist (Austin: University of Texas Press, 1981), pp. 13 and 15–16; and Frank Kermode, *The Sense of an Ending: Studies in the Theory of Fiction* (New York: Oxford University Press, 1967), pp. 38–41.

5. "Phaedrus," 276A in *Plato,* ed. Harold North Fruler (Cambridge: Harvard University Press, 1937), p. 267.

6. Gerald Graff, *Literature Against Itself: Literary Ideas in Modern Society* (Chicago: University of Chicago Press, 1979), pp. 193–94.

7. Jacques Derrida, *Writing and Difference,* trans. Alan Bass (Chicago: University of Chicago Press, 1978), p. 76.

8. Geoffrey H. Hartman, *Saving the Text: Literature/Derrida/Philosophy* (Baltimore: Johns Hopkins University Press, 1981), p. 66.

Chapter 5

1. Geoffrey H. Hartman, *Saving the Text*, p. 63.

2. Roland Barthes, *S/Z*, trans. Richard Miller (New York: Hill and Wang, 1974), pp. 4–15.

3. Mark C. Taylor, *Erring: A Postmodern A/theology* (Chicago: University of Chicago Press, 1984), p. 156.

4. Ibid., p. 28.

5. Ibid., p. 174.

6. Ibid., p. 116.

7. See Ralph Norman, "Necessary Texts: Pluralism and the Uses of Canon," *Soundings* (Fall 1987), pp. 236–46.

8. Albert C. Sundberg, Jr., *The Old Testament of the Early Church*, Harvard Theological Studies, no. 20 (Cambridge: Harvard University Press, 1964), and "Canon of the N.T.," in *The Interpreter's Dictionary of the Bible*, ed. Keith Crim, Supplementary volume (Nashville: Abingdon Press, 1976), pp. 136–40.

9. Jacques Derrida, "Structure, Sign and Play in the Discourse of the Human Sciences," in *The Languages of Criticism and the Sciences of Man: The Structuralist Controversy*, ed. Richard Macksey and Eugenio Donato (Baltimore: Johns Hopkins University Press, 1970), p. 271.

10. Roland Barthes, *The Pleasure of the Text*, trans. Richard Miller (New York: Hill and Wang, 1975).

11. Ibid., pp. 6–7 and 43.

12. Jonathan Culler, *Roland Barthes* (New York: Oxford University Press, 1983), p. 122.

13. Barthes, *S/Z*, p. 16.

14. Stanley Fish, *Is There a Text in This Class? The Authority of Interpretive Communities* (Cambridge: Harvard University Press, 1980), p. 14. See also his "Normal Circumstances, Literal Language, Direct Speech Acts, the Ordinary, the Everyday, the Obvious, What Goes Without Saying, and Other Special Cases," in *Interpretive Social Sciences: A Reader*, ed. Paul Rabinow and William M. Sullivan (Berkeley: University of California Press, 1979).

15. Roland Barthes, *Mythologies*, trans. Annette Lavers (New York: Hill and Wang, 1972).

16. See Alan C. Golding, "A History of American Poetry Anthologies," in *Canons*, ed. Robert von Hallberg (Chicago: University of Chicago Press, 1984), pp. 279–309.

17. See Charles Altieri, "An Idea and Ideal of a Literary Canon," in Ibid., pp. 41–64.

18. See Barbara Herrnstein Smith, "Contingencies of Value," in Ibid., pp. 5–41.

19. For such an analysis, see the Conclusion to my *Moral Fiber: Character and Belief in Recent American Fiction* (Philadelphia: Fortress Press, 1982).

20. James A. Sanders, *Canon and Community* (Philadelphia: Fortress Press, 1984), p. 36.

21. Herbert N. Schneidau, *Sacred Discontent: The Bible and Western Tradition* (Baton Rouge: Louisiana State University Press, 1976), p. 80.

Conclusion

1. Barthes, *Image-Music-Text*, pp. 83–84.

2. Taylor, *Erring*, p. 156.

3. Hugh Kenner, "The Making of the Modernist Canon," in *Canons*, ed. Robert von Hallberg, p. 373.

4. Fish, *Is There a Text in This Class?*, p. 320.

5. Ibid., p. 336.

6. David H. Kelsey, *The Uses of Scripture in Recent Theology* (Philadelphia: Fortress Press, 1975), p. 150.

7. Ibid., p. 170.

8. Hans W. Frei, *The Eclipse of Biblical Narrative: A Study in Eighteenth and Nineteenth Century Hermeneutics* (New Haven: Yale University Press, 1974), p. 130.

9. Ibid., p. 268.

10. Bernhard W. Anderson, *The Unfolding Drama of the Bible: Eight Studies Introducing the Bible as a Whole* (New York: Association Press, 1957).

11. C. H. Dodd, *The Authority of the Bible* (New York: Harper and Brothers, 1929), p. 31.

12. Ibid., p. 295.

13. Karl Barth, *Church Dogmatics*, vol. 1, *The Doctrine of the Word of God*, trans. G. T. Thomson (New York: Charles Scribner and Sons, 1936), p. 114.

14. Ibid., p. 117.

15. Ibid., p. 125.

16. David Tracy, *The Analogical Imagination: Christian Theology and the Culture of Pluralism* (New York: Crossroad, 1981), p. 102.

17. Ibid., p. 114.

18. Ibid., p. 119.

19. Ibid., p. 255.

20. Ibid., p. 249.

21. Ibid., p. 263.

22. Ibid., p. 275.

23. Ibid., p. 276.

24. Thomas Paine, *The Age of Reason*, Part 1, *The Complete Religious and*

Theological Works of Thomas Paine (New York: Peter Eckler Publishing Co., 1922), p. 29.

25. Frank Kermode, "The Argument About Canons," in *The Bible and the Narrative Tradition,* ed. Frank McConnell, pp. 78–96.

26. Frank Kermode, *The Classic: Literary Images of Permanence and Change* (New York: Viking Press, 1975), pp. 15–16.

27. Ibid., p. 135.

28. Jane Tompkins, *Sensational Designs: The Cultural Work of American Fiction* (New York: Oxford University Press, 1985), pp. 4–5.

29. George Steiner, *Real Presences* (Cambridge: Cambridge University Press, 1986), p. 7.

Index